The Cultural Construction of International Relations

Also by Beate Jahn

POLITIK UND MORAL

The Cultural Construction of International Relations

The Invention of the State of Nature

Beate Jahn
Lecturer in International Relations
University of Sussex
Brighton

Published by
PALGRAVE MACMILLAN
Houndmills, Basingstoke, Hampshire RG21 6XS and
175 Fifth Avenue, New York, N.Y. 10010
Companies and representatives throughout the world

PALGRAVE MACMILLAN is the global academic imprint of the Palgrave Macmillan division of St. Martin's Press, LLC and of Palgrave Macmillan Ltd. Macmillan® is a registered trademark in the United States, United Kingdom and other countries. Palgrave is a registered trademark in the European Union and other countries.

Outside North America
ISBN-13: 978–0–333–80257–1
ISBN-10: 0–333–80257–8

Inside North America
ISBN: 0–312–23471–6

This book is printed on paper suitable for recycling and made from fully managed and sustained forest sources. Logging, pulping and manufacturing processes are expected to conform to the environmental regulations of the country of origin.

A catalogue record for this book is available from the British Library.

Library of Congress Catalog Card Number: 00–027114

Printed and bound in Great Britain by
CPI Antony Rowe, Chippenham and Eastbourne

To my parents

Contents

Acknowledgements

Without the very generous research grant which I have received for three years from the Deutsche Forschungsgemeinschaft (DFG) this book could not have been written. I am also indebted to Professor Volker Rittberger who has supported this project warmly. And I am grateful to Professor Lothar Brock who helped with innumerable references and made sure that I would not give up. Professor Gert Krell, too, has shown encouraging support and interest in the topic.

My parents, to whom this book is dedicated, have not only brought me up to think critically, but supported this project in every conceivable way. This book was written in four cities: Frankfurt, New York, London and Brighton. I would like to express my thanks to the friends and colleagues who have kept me company in those four cities. Andreas Scholz, Verena Schaedel and Gerard Holden in Frankfurt: Andreas Scholz brought treasures from second-hand book stores; he and Gerard Holden read an early version of the first part of this study and provided very helpful critical comments; and Verena Schaedel listened to endless tales about the Spaniards and the Amerindians. In New York, I would like to thank Peg Mulligan, David Perry, Dan Friel and Marion van Embricqs for being such wonderful friends; they kept me company during the solitary times of research in the library. In London, Martin Sharpe has distracted me with beautiful music and Julia Beusch and Claudia Buckenmaier regularly came to visit. Lucy Ford, Alex Colas, Zdenek Kavan and Julian Saurin have helped a lot to find my way around Sussex. Alex Colas has taken on some of my work in the last two months and thus given me space to finish the manuscript in time.

No one has helped as much as Justin Rosenberg, who has not only proofread the whole manuscript and endured my total absorption in the last two months, but the discussions we have had over the last four years have shaped my own thoughts deeply. His intellectual passion and clarity of mind have made their way into this study in such a way that now they can no longer be disentangled from my own thoughts.

Beate Jahn
Brighton

Introduction

This book tells a story, a story about the role of culture in International Relations. It is not, however, a straightforward story to tell, for mainstream International Relations theory, although it recognizes cultural diversity within humanity as one of the fundamental and defining problems of the international, nevertheless constructs the theory of International Relations on the basis of an apparent abstraction from that cultural diversity, namely the concept of the state of nature. Liberal as well as Realist International Relations theory attempts to cut across the problem of the cultural diversity of humanity not only by deriving its explanatory categories from this concept of the state of nature but also by grounding its policy advice on the assumption of a state of nature. This strategy is meant to achieve a theoretical as well as a practical aim. Any theory which aspires to making general statements about the interaction of culturally diverse actors in the world will confront the tension between its own claim to universal or general validity on the one hand, and the diverse, non-universal character of its subject matter on the other. The use of the concept of the state of nature, however, which presupposes a common, universal nature of human beings beneath their particular cultural identities, thus enables International Relations theory to make statements of general validity despite the cultural diversity of its subject matter.

Once posited, however, the assumption of a universal human nature also allows the discipline of International Relations to formulate practical political solutions to the problems generated by cultural diversity in the world based on nature. Hence, we find that for both Realists and Liberals *the* most important feature of human beings in the state of nature is reason. Reason, they assert, is common to all human beings irrespective of their particular cultural identities and can, therefore, be used to overcome the particularities and conflicts generated by cultural diversity. Reason, in the Realist account, does not only allow the scholar of International Relations to uncover and analyse the general and universal laws of international politics underneath their particular appearances, but it is also the means by which statesmen assess the international situation they are confronted with and on this basis interact with their counterparts; in this political practice, the statesmen, so to speak, rise above the cultural identities of their respective political communities and meet on the common and universal ground of reason. For Liberals, too, reason is the universal means inherent in and open to all human beings who can, therefore, by applying reason to the nature of human beings, derive certain universally valid principles of political organization. The realization and embodiment of these principles in the political organization of humanity, thus, will gradually overcome conflicts arising out of cultural diversity.

And this is the reason why the story about the role of culture in International Relations is not a straightforward one to tell. Because no sooner have we established that mainstream International Relations theory, indeed, takes the cultural diversity of humanity as a defining feature of its problematic, we find it leaving culture behind and grounding itself instead in a variety of versions of the concept of the state of nature. The starting point for my argument in this study, however, is the assumption that culture is an integral part of human nature – is, in fact, constitutive of human nature. If this assumption is correct, it follows that there cannot be a human nature apart from, or even in contrast to, culture. Any conception of human nature would then have to be taken as the expression of a culturally particular belief rather than as the universal roots as well as the universal *telos* of humanity, that is as an alternative to its cultural diversity. And as such, as a culturally particular discourse on human nature, it cannot be given *a priori* but must have been developed within a particular context as the answer to a concrete problem.

In Part I of this study I will trace the roots of this particular discourse on the concept of the state of nature, which plays such a crucial role in International Relations theory, back to the concrete intercultural encounter in the course of which it was developed in its modern sense. The encounter between Spaniards and Amerindian peoples in the course of the discovery of America challenged Spanish-Christian conceptions of human nature, history and destiny in their very foundations and forced the Spaniards to adjust their culturally peculiar conceptions in such a way that they could accommodate the existence of the Amerindian peoples. It was during this discourse on the nature of the Amerindian peoples that the Spaniards eventually used the old religious concept of the state of nature – namely the condition of human beings in the paradisical period before the fall from grace – and gave it new meaning by identifying the Amerindian peoples with that state of nature. This move, however, amounted to a considerable reinterpretation of the concept of the state of nature in that it now came to describe a secular and historical condition as the first stage of existence for all of humanity.

As I will demonstrate in Part II of this study, this explanation for the cultural difference between Amerindian and European societies, namely that the Amerindians represented human beings in the state of nature, went on to have far reaching implications for European social and political thought. First of all, since the discovery of the Amerindian peoples directly contradicted various biblical statements about the nature and history of humanity in the world, it gradually led to a relativization and, eventually, replacement of the traditional modes of constructing knowledge. Whereas traditionally knowledge was validly constructed by reading and interpreting an accepted canon of authoritative texts, social and historical knowledge were now to be gained through an empirical study of the nature of man and society. This, of course, meant the study of the Amerindian peoples who were thought to exhibit the nature of man and society in their purest, original form. Secondly, the assumption that the Amerindians represented the state of nature or, at any rate, an earlier stage of the historical development of humankind led to the construction of philosophies of history 'explaining' not only how and why human beings had moved out of this state of nature and developed cultures, but also justified this development as in the interest of all of humanity and, therefore, morally valid and necessary. Thirdly, however, since Europeans traditionally grounded their own societies on natural law and the Amerindian societies were taken to be governed almost entirely by nature, it was possible to derive some insight into the original natural law which might have been lost during the particular historical and cultural developments the European societies had taken. Since in the eyes of the European authors Amerindian societies were characterized by freedom and equality, based on the absence of government and private property, men were taken to be free and equal by nature. Political freedom and social equality, however, were conspicuously absent from European societies and were now taken as universally valid natural rights of human beings which had to be realized in any society claiming to be based on natural law. Thus, European reformers set out to criticize those aspects of their own societies which they took to be against natural law and developed blueprints for the organization of society in accordance with natural law. These blueprints, in turn, came to play an important role in the American and French Revolutions. The discovery of the Amerindian peoples and their identification with the state of nature, then, had gradually over a period of some three hundred years led to a redefinition of valid knowledge, the history of humanity and its destiny in the realization of commonwealths based on the newly discovered 'real' nature of man. Classical

European political and social thought, then, is based directly or indirectly on a variety of interpretations of the state of nature identified with and to be empirically studied among Amerindian peoples.

But this radical development did not only have implications for the 'domestic' European social and political thought but for its emerging conceptions of the international, too. For this philosophy of history starting from a universal state of nature and culminating in a particular form of political and social organization based on principles derived from this natural state posited the normative validity of the latter for all of humanity. As a result, different cultures were ranked on a linear scale of development according to their respective realization of and approximation to the universally valid form of political and social organization. That is, cultural differences were reinterpreted as developmental stages. The assumption of the universal validity of a certain form of domestic political organization derived from a universal state of nature, consequently, led to a conception of the international based on a hierarchy of cultures. And this, as I will demonstrate in the conclusion to this book, is still the case in contemporary mainstream International Relations theory.

To tell the story of the role of culture in International Relations in this way means to argue against two commonly held beliefs. Firstly, in tracing the origins of the modern concept of the state of nature back to its roots it becomes apparent that the common representation of modern political and social thought, domestic and international, as an endogenously European cultural development denies and suppresses – often unconsciously, to be sure – the impact which the interaction with non-European cultures has had on its constitution. Whereas generally these ideas are taken to have originated, developed and, eventually, also to have been practised within the European context from where they were subsequently exported into the wider world, this study argues that there is a definite reverse undercurrent in which these ideas and the resulting practices have actually been developed in the context of the systematic interaction between European and non-European cultures, that is imported from an international encounter into domestic political thought and practice from where they were subsequently exported again into the international realm. Secondly, in reconstructing the definite course the concept of the state of nature has taken from its identification with the Amerindian peoples through domestic European political and social thought to the theory of International Relations, this study contradicts the commonly held belief that the distinction between political and international theory is based on, and justified with respect to, a basic difference between the 'nature' of international politics and the 'nature' of domestic politics. Not only does this study demonstrate that both political and international theory are derived from the same conception of the state of nature but also that a key element of the separation between the two disciplines is historically the result of different kinds of moral and legal principles which the Europeans applied to the different 'stages of development', in the form of culturally diverse societies, with which they found themselves coexisting in a single historical time.

In telling this story about the cultural origins of the concept of the state of nature, however, another story unfolds before our eyes. And this is a story about the power of culture in the theory and practice of European politics. For the development sketched out above led to a radical transformation of European political thought, domestic and international, whose origins and concrete political meaning is not open to reflection and examination any longer. That is, the assumption of a natural state of man devoid of cultural development has, as the basis for a new epistemology, pervaded European political thought so thoroughly that it is not even any longer identified with concrete peoples or historical events. It has become a theoretical device, a hypothetical state of nature which is considered to be 'neutral' and, above all, independent of any concrete historical contents. However, in going back to its origin in a concrete intercultural encounter which was itself highly charged with political, social and moral meaning, it is not only possible to examine its validity, that is to examine whether Amerindian peoples could with any justification be described as peoples without culture. But, more importantly, this historical analysis demonstrates that at no point in time was this concept only a theoretical device. It was developed in the course of the concrete interaction between Spaniards and Amerindians, it played a crucial role in European and North American domestic as well as international political practice and, as I will show in the conclusion, it still does so in Western foreign policies.

The power of culture consists, then, of two different but closely interrelated processes. On the one hand, it is the culturally peculiar definition of human nature, history and destiny which defines the framework, the outer limits and the internal possibilities of our understanding of the world and of ourselves and our role in it. And in the case of the discipline of International Relations this understanding is clearly based on a universal conception of human nature and, because of the hidden origins of this concept, a blissful unawareness of its particularist cultural identity and, therefore, its limited validity. On the other hand, then, the power of culture consists in political practice, not caused by but based on this particular cultural framework, its possibilities and limitations. The limitations of this cultural framework do not lead only to the reproduction of contradictory accounts of the 'nature' of international politics but also to a cyclical reproduction of international politics in practice.

For if it is true, as suggested in this study, that culture is constitutive of human nature rather than a deviation from it, meaning that human beings are for their interaction with each other, as well as with their natural environment, dependent on culture which organizes and directs and gives meaning to these activities in specific ways, then the discipline of International Relations would indeed do well to get rid of the concept of the state of nature and the theories based on it. It may well be necessary, then, to attempt the construction of a theory of International Relations on the assumption that there is no human nature without culture and that, consequently, a theory of International Relations has to inquire into the conditions of conflict and cooperation between cultures and into the political implications of a world in which cultures are, indeed, mutually constitutive and subject to change, rather than on the assumption that nature will one day overcome culture.

Before I can start to tell the story of this book itself, however, I would like to clarify two points which might otherwise provide ground for misunderstanding. The first one is the frequent use of terms like 'the Amerindians' or 'Amerindian peoples' throughout this book. These terms do not express either my ignorance of the fact that there were and still are a multitude of native American cultures, nor a conscious or unconscious denigration of the dignity of these peoples and their cultures. In fact, this whole study is a passionate plea for the reversal of a theory and practice which abstracts from, and thus denigrates, cultural identities, be they native American, European or Chinese, as more or less grave deviations from true, that is natural, humanity. If I use these terms, it is because they do express precisely those abstractions which have flown into the concept of the state of nature. Indeed, it was not the case that either the Spaniards or classical thinkers were not aware of the existence of a multitude of cultures in America. Yet, the various definitions of the concept of the state of nature rest invariably on certain societal features which, if they existed in the first place, were abstracted from the roles they played in a given society and subsequently applied to Amerindian societies in general, with the notable exception, that is, of the Aztec and the Inca Empires.

And there is a second set of terms that can give rise to such mis-understanding, namely 'man', 'men', 'mankind'. In the beginning of my research on this topic I intended to devote considerable space to the analysis of the gendered definition of the state of nature, that is to the fact that classical thinkers have actually consciously and openly defined 'true' humanity, the natural essence of humanity, as male. In addition, the fact that the contemporary authors I am going to quote in this study nevertheless use 'nature' as a neutral and universal concept over and against culture or gender, only demonstrates that my argument about the relationship between nature and culture has much deeper and wider implications. However, lack of space, unfortunately, has prevented a thorough analysis of the gendered contents of the state of nature. I have chosen to use the terms 'man', 'mankind' throughout this book on the one hand because they are the terms frequently used in the quotations by classical as well as contemporary authors, and on the other because they describe exactly what the authors mean, namely men.

The most happy of mortals should I think myself could I contribute to make mankind recover from their prejudices. By prejudices I here mean, not that which renders men ignorant of some particular things, but whatever renders them ignorant of themselves.

(Montesquieu, *The Spirit of the Laws*)

1
Culture, Nature and the Ambivalence of International Theory

For Francis Fukuyama the 'universalization of Western liberal democracy' after the end of the Cold War marks the end of history understood as 'mankind's ideological evolution' (1989: 4). This statement does not, however, imply that 'all societies become successful liberal societies, merely that they end their ideological pretensions of representing different and higher forms of human society' (1989: 13). There will, therefore, still be international conflicts among those who have not yet become successful liberal societies as well as between the latter and those who have already passed into the post-historical phase; but we do not have to concern ourselves with 'every crackpot messiah around the world, but only [with] those that are embodied in important social or political forces and movements, and which are therefore part of world history' (1989: 9). International conflicts, on this reading, are at least partly caused by different 'ideologies', different ideas about how society should be organized. Yet, we do not have to analyse these ideologies or their role in international politics as long as they are not embodied in powerful social and political forces.

Samuel Huntington, meanwhile, proclaims that the end of the Cold War marks the beginning of a period in which clashes of civilizations will be the major form of international conflict. He, too, then identifies civilizations, ideologies, belief systems as a major source of conflict and, unlike Fukuyama, insists that the discipline of International Relations should pay more attention to the cultural and religious beliefs, sensibilities and interests of other civilizations (Huntington, 1993: 49). But since, according to Huntington, the power of non-Western civilizational blocs, in particular that of the Islamic–Confucian bloc, has risen

1

considerably and is already threatening the position of the West, the main focus of his article and his advice for practitioners is to defend the Western position of economic and military superiority by all means – including the deliberate aggravation of conflicts between Islamic and Confucian states and intervention into those states' internal affairs in support of groups sympathetic to Western values (1993: 48f.).

Although this latter advice may not, in fact, be the most successful way of paying attention to the cultural sensibilities of non-Western peoples, what is of interest in the context of this study is the startling puzzle of two authors belonging to the opposite camps of mainstream IR theory, Realism and Liberalism, finding themselves not only in such close agreement but, furthermore, providing such a contradictory starting point for the student of international politics. For, on the one hand, both identify cultural differences as a major source of international conflicts in the contemporary world, and on the other, neither of them concludes that international relations has to concern itself thoroughly with the role of cultural difference in international politics. Moreover, the only hint of an explanation for this inconsistency seems to be the power relations in the world: because non-liberal ideas are not backed up with enough power, we do not have to study them, according to Fukuyama, while for Huntington they have already accumulated too much power so that we have to postpone the study of non-Western ideas until the West has managed to secure its position of economic and military superiority. What I am going to show in this chapter, however, is that this inconsistency, between the significance accorded to cultural difference and the unwillingness to study it, is neither dependent on a particular balance of power at a particular point in time, nor on the sophistication, or lack thereof, of the authors in question. Rather, it is inbuilt into the fundamental theoretical fabric of mainstream International Relations theory. A thorough investigation of Liberal and Realist theories of International Relations will show that both strands of thought identify cultural diversity as a major, if not *the* major, problematic of international politics and, furthermore, that both attempt to solve the problem of culture by returning to nature or, more specifically, by constructing their theories of International Relations on the assumption of a state of nature.

Culture

Since the discipline of International Relations does not provide a satisfactory definition of culture[1] it makes sense to go searching for it in that discipline which concerns itself, so to speak, professionally with culture: cultural anthropology. In the 1970s Clifford Geertz discussed the shortcomings of common concepts of culture in anthropology and offered an alternative. During the Enlightenment, he argued, two different and opposing views on culture were developed in the West. The first saw culture as temporary fashions, opinions and customs super-imposed on a universal human nature. This understanding was count-ered at the time by a second, historicist conception of culture in which man 'dissolves, without residue, into his time and place, a child and a perfect captive of his age' (Geertz, 1993: 37). The first, the evolutionary concept of culture, is unsatisfying and dangerous, says Geertz, because it denies truth and value to men as they are in their particular and con-crete cultural forms. And so is the second, the historicist concept of culture, because in it humanity becomes 'as various in its essence as it is in its expression' (1993: 37). Anthropology, therefore, in its attempt to avoid both these pitfalls has produced various forms of what Geertz calls the 'stratigraphic' concept of culture in which 'man is a composite of "levels", each superimposed upon those beneath it and underpinning those above it. As one analyses man, one peels off layer after layer, each such layer being complete and irreducible in itself, revealing another, quite different sort of layer underneath' (1993: 37). Thus, one peels off the layer of culture and finds a layer of structural and functional regular-ities beneath which there is a layer of psychological factors itself resting on the biological foundations of human life (1993: 37). But this solu-tion, too, has its problems. On the one hand, the attempt to find and define those universals underlying the particular cultural forms through 'public-opinion polling of the world's peoples in search of a *consensus gentium*' only leads back to the relativism which was to be avoided (1993: 40). On the other hand, once the different layers have been separated it is extremely difficult to reintegrate them, a difficulty which commonly leads to 'merely a placing of supposed facts from the cultural and subcultural levels side by side so as to induce a vague sense that some kind of relationship between them...obtains' (1993: 42). Geertz, therefore, sets out to replace this 'stratigraphic' conception 'of the relations between the various aspects of human existence with a synthetic one; that is, one in which biological, psychological, sociolo-gical, and cultural factors can be treated as variables within unitary systems of analysis' (1993: 44).

Geertz's alternative concept of culture entails two fundamental ideas. Rather than following the conventional understanding of culture as concrete patterns of behaviour such as 'customs, usages, traditions, habit clusters', Geertz proposes to see culture as 'a set of control mechanisms – plans, recipes, rules, instructions . . . – for the governing of behavior'; and he contends that 'man is precisely the animal most desperately dependent upon such extragenetic, outside-the-skin control mechanisms, such cultural programs for ordering his behavior' (1993: 44). Traditionally, it was assumed that biological man was completed before any kind of cultural development began. Geertz, however, points out that there are over a million years of overlap between man's immediate progenitors and the emergence of what we call *homo sapiens*, during the course of which cultural or protocultural activity was very much present. Indeed, 'the bulk of the biological changes that produced modern man . . . took place in the central nervous system and most especially in the brain' and it has become clear now that 'man is, in physical terms, an incomplete, an unfinished animal; that what sets him off most graphically from nonmen is less his sheer ability to learn (great as that is) than how much and what particular sorts of things he *has* to learn before he is able to function at all' (1993: 46). This considerable overlap in which cultural activity took place while biological man had not yet come into being suggests, argues Geertz, that 'culture, rather than being added on, so to speak, to a finished or virtually finished animal, was ingredient, and centrally ingredient, in the production of that animal itself' (1993: 47).

> Between the cultural pattern, the body, and the brain, a positive feedback system was created in which each shaped the progress of the other, a system in which the interaction among increasing tool use, the changing anatomy of the hand, and the expanding representation of the thumb on the cortex is only one of the more graphic examples. By submitting himself to governance by symbolically mediated programs for producing artifacts, organizing social life, or expressing emotions, man determined, if unwittingly, the culminating stages of his own biological destiny. Quite literally, though quite inadvertently, he created himself.
>
> (Geertz, 1993: 48)

This understanding of culture suggests that there is no such thing as 'human nature independent of culture'; in fact, because man lacks the biological instincts of animals he is dependent on their cultural production, for 'undirected by cultural patterns – organized systems of significant symbols – man's behavior would be virtually ungovernable, a mere chaos of pointless acts and exploding emotions, his experience virtually shapeless' (Geertz, 1993: 49, 46). Hence, if there is no culture without man, there is certainly no man without culture. Geertz's understanding suggests that, rather than men being divided by different cultures, men are united by the need of culture. All men are the products as well as the producers of culture. Culture in the sense of organized systems of significant symbols is, in fact, what men have in common, even while the particular forms of these cultural systems divide humanity. So:

> Man is to be defined neither by his innate capacities alone ... nor by his actual behaviors alone ... but rather by the link between them, by the way in which the first is transformed into the second, his generic potentialities focused into his specific performances. ... This, neither an unchanging subcultural self nor an established cross-cultural consensus, is what we really have in common.
>
> (1993: 52)

I will take up this concept of culture as a preliminary starting point for two reasons. Firstly, since it takes all human life as a product of culture(s), it allows me to explore how culture lies at the heart of the problematic of International Relations irrespective of time and place. Secondly, since it maintains the freedom of human beings in producing and changing culture(s), it creates an opening for my central argument that Western thought on international relations has been considerably influenced, changed and developed by the encounter with Amerindian peoples. For the purposes of the study of the role of culture in international relations this concept has two substantive as well as methodological implications. The first is as follows:

> Human thought is ... both social and public – that its natural habitat is the house yard, the marketplace, and the town square. Thinking consists not of 'happenings in the head' (though happenings there and elsewhere are necessary for it to occur) but in a traffic of what have been called ... significant symbols – words for the most part but also gestures, drawings, musical sounds, mechanical devices like clocks, or natural objects like jewels – anything, in fact, that is disengaged from its mere actuality and used to impose meaning upon experience.
>
> (1993: 45)

If human thought is social, then the particular cultural meanings are worked out not only in the interaction between human beings within political communities but also between political communities. Hence, international relations would then be, among other things, relations producing and reproducing cultural meanings for all those involved. And if human thought is public, then we can find the significant symbols producing specific cultural meaning in the public domain. If the main function of culture is to produce meanings which help people to organize their lives with each other and in their natural environment, then we will find them reflected in societal organization and institutions of any kind, and in the 'symbolic dimension of social action – art, religion, ideology, science, law, morality, common sense' (1993: 30). The second implication of this concept of culture is that

> when seen as a set of symbolic devices for controlling behavior, extrasomatic sources of information, culture provides the link between what men are intrinsically capable of becoming and what they actually, one by one, in fact become. Becoming human is becoming individual, and we become individual under the guidance of cultural patterns, historically created systems of meaning in terms of which we give form, order, point, and direction to our lives. And the cultural patterns involved are not general but specific...
>
> (Geertz, 1993: 52)

This indicates the need to study culture as the framework in which political action, societal organization and moral direction are worked out in specific cases because it is the cultural framework which, as a producer of human beings, sets limits explaining their choices and actions, and as a product of human interaction it determines the possibilities and directions of change. It is important to note, though, that this framework is 'not a power, something to which social events, behaviors, institutions, or processes can be causally attributed; it is a context, something in which they can be intelligibly – that is, thickly – described' (Geertz, 1993: 14). It is equally important to point out that a cultural framework, though it has to be coherent to some extent, can and does contain all kinds of contradictions. It cannot be taken as an 'impeccable description of formal order in whose actual existence nobody can quite believe' (1993: 18).

What, then, does a cultural analysis consist of? It means to trace the 'curve of a social discourse'; it is because cultural forms find articulation in social action that we have to attend to behaviour, that we 'gain empirical access to them by inspecting events, not by arranging abstracted entities into unified patterns' (1993: 19, 17). But even if a 'cultural analysis is intrinsically incomplete' because a cultural framework can never be fully and comprehensibly described, this does not mean that the 'thick description' we provide of a cultural system does not have any implications beyond the particular case; on the contrary, 'it is the extension of our analyses to wider contexts that, along with their theoretical implications, recommends them to general attention and justifies our constructing them' (1993: 29, 21). For, of course, 'it is not necessary to know everything in order to understand something' (1993: 20).

And this is exactly what this study is trying to do. It attempts to trace the curve of a culturally specific – Western – public discourse on international politics and it provides a thick description of the roots of this discourse in a particular international conflict and its practice. In demonstrating the unreflected and culturally peculiar way in which the West has theoretically construed international politics over hundreds of years now, it attempts to show the power of culture as a producer even of as 'enlightened' a people as we are. And in analysing the conflict from which this modern understanding of international politics has developed it attempts to demonstrate our human capabilities of changing this particularly debilitating cultural conception of international politics.

Realism

'Society's forms are culture's substance', that is political action, social institutions and organizations, and moral beliefs are all arranged within cultural frameworks, they are the substance, the empirical and material embodiments of culture as a system of meanings. Concentrating on Hans Morgenthau, Hedley Bull and Kenneth Waltz I am going to show that culture in this sense plays a crucial role in Realist conceptions of the international.[2]

What, then, distinguishes the international from the domestic for these scholars? 'What factor making for peace and order exists within national societies which is lacking on the international scene? The answer seems obvious – it is the state itself' (Morgenthau, 1993: 333). Similarly, Bull contends that 'the starting point for international relations is the existence of *states*, or independent political communities' (Bull, 1977: 8) and Waltz holds that 'government is . . . a precondition for society' (Waltz, 1959: 227f). The difference between the domestic and the international spheres, then, appears to be the presence of government in the former and its absence in the latter. Yet, the overwhelming power of the state is actually not enough to establish peace and order in the domestic realm as the frequency and destructiveness of civil wars clearly demonstrate (Morgenthau, 1993: 340), and Waltz, too, points out that the domestic is just as much prone to violence as the international – in fact, civil wars may 'be bloodier' than wars among states (Waltz, 1979: 103). For Bull, the precondition of any social life is order but 'the order which men look for in social life is not *any* pattern or regularity in the relations of human individuals or groups, but a pattern that leads to a particular result, an arrangement of social life such that it promotes certain goals or values' (Bull, 1977: 4). And we do find order also in 'primitive stateless societies' (1977: 59) so that the existence of the state as such, all three authors eventually agree, cannot explain the difference between the domestic and the international.

What, then, is it that we have to add to the existence of government or the state that distinguishes the domestic from the international? Morgenthau holds that in addition to the overwhelming power of the state two other conditions pertain in the domestic sphere which are equally important for the establishment of peace and order, namely suprasectional loyalties within the population and an expectation of justice guaranteed by the state (1993: 334). Despite all kinds of diverse interests and associational divisions within society, its members share what we might clearly call a national culture.

> They partake of the same language, the same customs, the same historic recollections, the same fundamental social and political philosophy, the same national symbols. They read the same newspapers, listen to the same radio programs, observe the same holidays, and worship the same heroes. Above all, they compare their own nation with other nations and realize how much more they have in common with each other than with members of the other nations. ... Their intellectual convictions and moral valuations derive from that membership.
>
> (Morgenthau, 1993: 335f.)

These suprasectional loyalties are interpersonally shared practices, beliefs and values – culture – which can either cement peace and order in society or become potent weapons in social conflicts. And it is at this point that societal institutions like public opinion, elections, parliamentary votes or examination boards come into play which provide means to arbitrate between these conflicting claims. Most of these institutions are provided by the state and since all the members of society recognize those rules and institutions as binding they provide a mechanism for peaceful change. On the one hand, these institutions and rules are justified within the cultural framework of the society; on the other, all groups can rely on the chance, at some point, to advance their own conception of justice. Hence, within the domestic realm there is an expectation of the attainment of justice (Morgenthau, 1993: 337). And it is only on the basis of this cultural consensus and these societal institutions allowing for the expectation of justice that the state with its overwhelming power comes in as a third factor (1993: 337). There is absolutely no question for Morgenthau that the state is not an 'artificial creation' imposed upon society but an integral part of society, the creation of society (1993: 340).

For Waltz, too, government only establishes 'the conditions for peace', not peace itself (1959: 227f). That is, 'a government, ruling by some standard of legitimacy, arrogates to itself the right to use force – that is, to apply a variety of sanctions to control the use of force by its subjects' (Waltz, 1979: 103). This mode of organization enables the units within society 'to specialize, to pursue their own interests without concern for developing the means of maintaining their identity and preserving their security in the presence of others' (1979: 104). 'National politics', then, 'is the realm of authority, of administration, and of law' (1979: 104). And these rest on the legitimacy they have in the eyes of the population, while dissenters are also carried along by two considerations: either their judgement that they do not have enough power to change decisions made, or their conviction, 'based on perceived interest and customary loyalty, that in the long run it is to their advantage to go along with the national decision and work in the prescribed and accepted ways for its change' (Waltz, 1959: 177f). The better the state, 'or, we can now add, the more nationalistic', the more it can rely on the agreement of its citizens (Waltz, 1959: 178). In addition, like Morgenthau, Waltz holds that feelings of national loyalty and identification with the state are also powerfully reinforced by international crises (1959: 179).

Even more for Hedley Bull than for Morgenthau and Waltz, the precondition for social life seems to be the acceptance of certain kinds of values. Three of these values or goals in particular, although by no means the only ones, Bull identifies as elementary, primary and universal. Life, truth and property are elementary goals, he argues, because 'a constellation of persons or groups among whom there existed no expectation of security against violence, or the honouring of agreements or of stability of possession we should hardly call a society at all' (Bull, 1977: 5). These values or goals are also primary because, in Bull's opinion, they are the precondition for the pursuit of any further goals, and they are universal because they seem to be promoted by all actual societies (1977: 5f). Hence, the defining feature of a society is not the state but that its members share at least those basic values.

Therefore, 'without the state's contribution there can be no domestic peace, but with nothing but the state's contribution there can be no domestic peace either' (Morgenthau, 1993: 339). With this statement, I think, Bull and Waltz would have to agree. Less adamant than Morgenthau and Waltz about the indispensability of the state, Bull elaborates at length that the most basic feature of a domestic society must be the acceptance of certain common values. And Waltz leaves no doubt either that law, authority and administration rest upon some kind of legitimacy backed up by the power of the state. A domestic society, then, is a group of individuals who share certain values and organize their lives around institutions based upon and upholding these values. In short, a society is a cultural community.

And what distinguishes the domestic from the international is the fact that the individual members of humanity do not constitute a society in that sense. For Morgenthau, humanity is divided into nations characterized by different moral and political values and it would require a 'revaluation of all values', an 'unprecedented moral and political revolution' to replace the allegiance of individuals to their nation with an allegiance to humanity (Morgenthau, 1993: 341). In other words, because of the lack of cultural unity among humankind, society cannot exist on a global scale and, hence, there can be no global political organization of humanity, that is, there can be no world state. Under the present conditions, 'lacking moral and political consensus', a global political organization of mankind would be permanently threatened by civil war and could, thus, not provide the peace the domestic political organization, by and large, does provide (1993: 342). International peace cannot be permanently established without a world state and the latter is impossible without 'a world community willing and able to support it' (1993: 342f). Whereas the members of a domestic society do not have to maintain their identity and preserve their security, this is exactly what states as actors in the international sphere have to do (Waltz, 1979: 104). In contrast to domestic life as the 'realm of authority, of administration, and of law, international politics is the realm of power, of struggle, and of accommodation' (1979: 113).

At this point it may appear as if Bull would clearly depart from the other two for, after all, he argues that the international sphere can be described as a *society*, albeit an anarchic one, by which he means 'a group of states, conscious of certain common interests and common values . . . in the sense that they conceive themselves to be bound by a common set of rules in their relations with one another, and share in the working of common institutions' (1977: 13). However, there remain for him two crucial differences between a domestic and an international society. First of all, Bull contends that the members of the international society are *states* and not *individuals* (1977: 8). And he rejects the domestic analogy and maintains that 'states, after all, are very unlike human individuals' – there is a qualitative difference between a society made up of states and one made up of individuals (1977: 49).

The second major difference between domestic societies and the international society is the fact that the values and rules by which the members of the international society feel themselves bound are 'primitive' compared to those shared by the members of a domestic society. They are 'primitive' because they are the basic values which make societal life possible in the first place. But 'modern international society. . . is culturally heterogeneous' in the sense that the domestic societies, the states, which make up the international system have developed and do rest on more than just those basic values (1977: 64). And these secondary values make modern international society culturally heterogeneous. Indeed, Bull himself clearly states that even 'primitive stateless societies are marked by a high degree of cultural homogeneity' while the society of sovereign states 'is *par excellence* a society that is culturally heterogeneous' (1977: 64). Hence, despite Bull's insistence that there are societal elements, shared values, to be found in the international sphere, he does assume that in the past as well as in the future 'there will be constant change and variety in the ideologies that are espoused in different parts of the world' and he concludes that precisely for this reason

> the attempt to remould a states system on principles of ideological fixity and uniformity is likely to be a source of disorder, and we are driven back to the principle that order is best founded upon agreement to tolerate ideological difference, namely the principle upon which the present states system is founded.
>
> (Bull, 1977: 248)

Hence, despite Bull's insistence on elements of society – shared values and rules – in the international sphere, he, too, sees the major difference between the international and the domestic in the fact that the former is characterized by cultural diversity.

If, then, the international is constituted essentially by culturally heterogeneous political communities as opposed to culturally more or less
homogeneous individuals in the domestic sphere we would expect the
analysis of the conditions of conflict and cooperation between cultures
to lie at the heart of a realist theory of international relations. However,
what we find is quite the opposite. In constructing the major com-
ponents of International Relations theory, all the authors take pains to
eliminate any trace of cultural diversity. Morgenthau insists that a
'rational outline', or 'map' is necessary to order and give meaning to
the infinite number of facts available to us (1993: 4f). The fundamental
problem of cultural diversity, however, is not reflected in the 'rational
outline', the 'map' suggested. On the contrary, the 'concept of interest
defined in terms of power' as the 'main signpost' for a realist theory of
international relations 'sets politics as an autonomous sphere of action
and understanding apart from other spheres, such as economics...,
ethics, aesthetics, or religion' (Morgenthau, 1993: 5). In fact, Morgenthau maintains, international politics is by definition power politics.
Irrespective of the ultimate goals defined in religious, economic, philosophic, or social terms, the immediate goal of international politics, he
holds, is always power. Although these ultimate goals may be pursued in
all kinds of ways and by different means, it is only if they are pursued by
striving for power that we talk about international politics (1993: 29).

And this power struggle is the rational kernel of international politics,
it is what a scholar of international relations analyses. Morgenthau
emphasizes that not all interaction between independent political communities or states is political, that is if two nations exchange goods for
the purpose of gaining wealth, or if two nations negotiate an extradition
treaty, or if nations provide relief from natural catastrophes, they are not
engaged in a struggle for power, understood as 'man's control over the
minds and actions of other men', and, hence, not engaged in international politics (1993: 29f). By defining international politics as
power politics Morgenthau has actually excluded all those aspects of
human life and social relations which are determined by their cultural
identities, which, in fact, constitute the state or independent political
community as an actor in world politics in the first place. Economic
relations between nations, cultural exchange between nations, even
international military policies, are not the subject of a theory of international relations if they are not undertaken for the purpose of a power
struggle (1993: 34).

Likewise, Waltz starts his *Theory of International Politics* by contending
that 'in reality, everything is related to everything else, and one domain

cannot be separated from others. Theory isolates one realm from all others in order to deal with it intellectually. To isolate a realm is a precondition to developing a theory that will explain what goes on within it' (1979: 8). In order to be successful, then, 'a theory has to show how international politics can be conceived of as a domain distinct from the economic, social, and other international domains that one may conceive of' (Waltz, 1979: 79). This can be done, according to Waltz, by employing a systemic theory which defines the structure of the international realm. So the anarchic structure of the international realm 'entails relations of coordination among a system's units, and that implies their sameness' (1979: 93).

> In defining international-political structures we take states with whatever traditions, habits, objectives, desires, and forms of government they may have. We do not ask whether states are revolutionary or legitimate, authoritarian or democratic, ideological or pragmatic. We abstract from every attribute of states except their capabilities. Nor in thinking about structure do we ask about the relations of states – their feelings of friendship and hostility, their diplomatic exchanges, the alliances they form, and the extent of the contacts and exchanges among them. We ask what range of expectations arises merely from looking at the type of order that prevails among them and at the distribution of capabilities within that order. We abstract from any particular qualities of states and from all of their concrete connections. What emerges is a positional picture, a general description of the ordered overall arrangement of a society written in terms of the placement of units rather than in terms of their qualities.
>
> (Waltz, 1979: 99)

Having abstracted from all the particulars of the units or actors we can see that their sameness is just as much preserved by the structure of the system as it originated in their constitution, because in the anarchic international sphere all the actors have to protect themselves and their identity against others, simply because there is no institution which will do it for them. Hence, 'in anarchic realms, like units coact. . . . In an anarchic realm the units are functionally similar and tend to remain so' (Waltz 1979: 104f). But if the actors in the international sphere are like units, what do we study? We distinguish between them in terms of their capabilities to perform the function of providing security, that is we analyse their power in relation to the power of other actors in the system (1979: 97). For Bull, too, states as actors in the international sphere become 'like units'. They are 'independent political communities, each of which possesses a government and asserts sovereignty in relation to a particular portion of the earth's surface and a particular segment of the human population' (Bull, 1977: 8). Bull's insistence on shared rules and values in the international sphere do not relativize this treatment of states as 'like units' precisely because he asserts that those rules and values are shared by all of them. Consequently, he distinguishes between states in the international sphere with respect to their power (1977: 107f, 92f).

Hence, 'if there is any distinctively political theory of international politics, balance-of-power theory is it' and 'a balance-of-power theory, properly stated, begins with assumptions about states: They are unitary actors who, at a minimum, seek their own preservation and, at a maximum, drive for universal domination' (Waltz, 1979: 117f). Likewise, Morgenthau comes to the conclusion that peace and order, or stability, can be achieved in the international sphere by balance of power politics. For balance of power politics maintains the stability of the system and the survival of the elements composing it. Under conditions of anarchy, balance of power politics is necessary to preserve the survival of those units that make up society in the first place – individuals – or of units which are entitled to survival because they protect those basic individual units – states (Morgenthau, 1993: 185). And Bull holds that 'the chief function of the balance of power... is not to preserve peace, but to preserve the system of states itself' (Bull, 1977: 107), and that 'international law depends for its very existence as an operating system of rules on the balance of power' even if those rules are frequently broken (1977: 109).

These approaches raise the questions how and why Realists attempt to construct the theory of International Relations on 'like units' and power relations in light of the fact that previously they had established that the international system was characterized by culturally unlike units. For Morgenthau, there is no question that the laws of politics have their roots in a universal human nature which underlies cultural particularity (1993: 4). Although, on the one hand, the events we analyse are unique, on the other hand, they are similar because they are manifestations of social forces and 'social forces are the product of human nature in action' (Morgenthau, 1993: 19). Thus, we have a contingent and a universal element in international politics. Following Hobbes, Morgenthau maintains that there are three biopsychological drives inherent in human nature, namely the drives to live, to propagate and to dominate, which in turn create society (1993: 36f). And because these drives are inherent in human nature 'it is sufficient to state that the struggle for power is universal in time and space' (1993: 36, 67n).

The contingent element is the development of different kinds of societies based on different cultures, civilizations, or ideologies whose existence is also necessary, according to Morgenthau, because the untamed struggle for power as such is self-destructive (1993: 220). Hence, all successful societies have to pacify and regulate these power drives in order to survive. The automatic forms of behaviour by which individuals adhere to the standards and rules their society has developed to restrain and pacify their power aspirations can be called civilization (1993: 222). As the basis for a theory of international relations, however, these societal and cultural developments are not useful because they are temporally and spatially relative. That is, cultural and moral principles change over time and they differ from one society to the next (1993: 246). In addition, Morgenthau considers the modern development of societies based on national cultures as one of the most dangerous threats to peace and order in the world, because each nation is convinced that its own values and ideals provide the basis for a salvation of all of humanity and, thus, embarks on sacred missions to impose them on others (1993: 245). Culture, therefore, is not only a contingent concept because it changes over time and from place to place; it is also a dangerous one because the political practice based on these cultural convictions have become a major threat to peace.

No wonder, then, that Morgenthau turns to the one truly universal and timeless principle, power, as the basis for a general theory of international politics. And this principle is the power drive inherent in human nature which can be detected even if

> frequently its basic manifestations do not appear as what they actually are – manifestations of a struggle for power. Rather, the element of power as the immediate goal of the policy pursued is explained and justified in ethical, legal, or biological terms. That is to say: the true nature of the policy is concealed by ideological justifications and rationalizations.
>
> (Morgenthau, 1993: 99)

A realist theory of international relations, then, is basically the attempt to uncover the 'true nature' of international politics, and since cultural justifications and rationalizations are just superimposed on 'true human nature' their study cannot provide the basis for a general theory of international relations.

In a similar vein, Waltz attempts to base the theory of international politics on nature. Only, he is not inspired by Hobbes but rather by Rousseau.

> Because of the difficulty of knowing such a thing as a pure human nature, because the human nature we do know reflects both man's nature and the influence of his environment, definitions of human nature such as those of Spinoza and Hobbes are arbitrary and can lead to no valid social or political conclusions. Theoretically at least one can strip away environmentally acquired characteristics and arrive at a view of human nature itself. Rousseau himself has advanced 'certain arguments, and risked some conjectures,' to this end.
>
> (Waltz, 1959: 166)

Rousseau held that human beings in the state of nature have no need to cooperate and argued that as a consequence they lived a solitary life. They could satisfy their basic needs without the help of others. In order to exemplify this point, Rousseau told the parable of the stag hunt which Waltz picks up and reinterprets. Whereas for Rousseau the parable expressed that human beings in the state of nature did not *need* to cooperate (for there were hares for all of them), Waltz's interpretation of this parable is that people in the state of nature *cannot* cooperate (1959: 167f). It is, in Waltz's interpretation, the absence of government in the state of nature which makes every individual hunter rather go for his hare than the common stag. For Waltz, a theory of international relations studies the recurrence of consequences, in this case, of war, and for this reason has to concentrate on the common, timeless, general structures of the world, rather than the contingent and particular ones (1959: 4f).

> Each state pursues its own interests, however defined, in ways it judges best. Force is a means of achieving the external ends of states because there exists no consistent, reliable process of reconciling the conflicts of interest that inevitably arise among similar units in a condition of anarchy. A foreign policy based on this image of international relations is neither moral nor immoral, but embodies merely a reasoned response to the world about us.
>
> (Waltz, 1959: 238)

The attraction which Rousseau has for Waltz stems from the fact that 'Rousseau ... makes possible a theory of international relations that in

general terms explains the behavior of all states, whether good or bad'
(1959: 182f).

And such a theory must be built on some understanding of nature
for Hedley Bull, as well. Bull rejects the Hobbesian and the Kantian
version of the state of nature and opts for Locke's understanding as
coming closest to what we find in the international sphere (Bull, 1977:
26f, 47f).

> If, then, we are to compare international relations with an imagined,
> pre-contractual state of nature among individual men, we may well
> choose not Hobbes's description of that condition but Locke's.
> Locke's conception of the state of nature as a society without govern-
> ment does in fact provide us with a close analogy with the society of
> states. In modern international society, as in Locke's state of nature,
> there is no central authority able to interpret and enforce the law, and
> thus individual members of the society must themselves judge and
> enforce it. Because in such a society each member of it is a judge in
> his own cause, and because those who seek to enforce the law do not
> always prevail, justice in such a society is crude and uncertain. But
> there is nevertheless a great difference between such a rudimentary
> form of social life and none at all.
>
> (Bull, 1977: 48)

Here, as in Morgenthau and Waltz, the particular understanding of
the state of nature provides Bull with certain kinds of universal features
to be found in international society and, thus, enables him to build a
theory of international relations on those fundamental, recurrent features of social life rather than on the problematic of cultural diversity
and historical change which had been identified as the central problem
of the international sphere.

The concept of the state of nature, then, provides us with an answer to
the question how Realists get from cultural diversity to uniform power
politics. In using the concept of the state of nature they assume that
there is, indeed, a deeper level than that of cultural diversity. And this
deeper level, a universal one, allows a realist theory of International
Relations to make 'general' statements, statements that are relevant for
more than a particular (intercultural) conflict in space and time. Realist
understanding of theory, and of the tasks of theory, then, is one reason
for this move. The belief in the objectivity of the laws of politics makes a
theory which reflects these objective laws possible (Morgenthau, 1993:
4; Waltz, 1979: 6). Rationality lies in the lawlike character, in the

recurrence or repetition of certain kinds of behaviour under similar circumstances and not with 'irrational elements'.

Yet a theory of foreign policy which aims at rationality must for the time being, as it were, abstract from . . . irrational elements and seek to paint a picture of foreign policy which presents the rational essence to be found in experience, without the contingent deviations from rationality which are also found in experience. Deviations from rationality which are not the result of the personal whim or the personal psychopathology of the policy maker may appear contingent only from the vantage point of rationality, but may themselves be elements in a coherent system of irrationality. The possibility of constructing, as it were, a counter-theory of irrational politics is worth exploring.

(Morgenthau, 1993: 7)

Interestingly enough, there are two elements to be found in experience, in reality, a rational and an irrational one. The rational one is derived from nature – the nature of the individual or the international environment – the irrational one, which according to Morgenthau could also build a coherent system, would then be what is not nature but culture, individual whims and psychopathologies, any concrete and particular phenomenon in time and space. Similarly, Bull is quite happy to remark that

there does in fact exist a close connection between order in the sense in which it is defined here, and the conformity of conduct to scientific laws that afford a basis for predicting future behaviour. One of the consequences of a situation in which elementary or primary goals of social coexistence are consistently upheld is that regular patterns of behaviour become known, are formulated as general laws, and afford a basis for expectations about future behaviour.

(Bull, 1977: 7)

What is interesting is that in all these cases rationality is found and founded in nature, in the natural recurrence of certain kinds of behaviour, in the natural laws which apply under certain kinds of conditions. But this is by no means an amoral or immoral theory because rationality is clearly positive, it is the means the realist authors attempt to employ in order to point towards ways of overcoming or at least containing war, instability and irrationality. And this belief is another and much more important reason for the Realist approach to international politics via the state of nature rather than the diversity of cultures. For, after all, nature provides a common, universal basis for an otherwise, culturally, hopelessly divided humanity. Therefore, the only moral approach to international politics is a rational one.

> Aware of the inevitable gap between good – that is, rational – foreign policy and foreign policy as it actually is, political realism maintains not only that theory must focus upon the rational elements of political reality, but also that foreign policy ought to be rational in view of its own moral and practical purposes.
>
> (Morgenthau, 1993: 10)

Liberalism

There is, then, a morality in Realist International Relations theory based on rationality: reason itself, which in turn is common to all human beings derived from their nature. This, it seems, is not good enough for Liberals[3] who contend that the uncritical acceptance of the 'conception of the world developed by Hobbes' results in 'insufficient attention to a variety of philosophically interesting and practically important normative problems of international relations' (Beitz, 1979: vii). They set out, therefore, to stress or open up those areas of moral choice which they accuse Realism of having overlooked. Hence, Beitz attempts 'to work out a more satisfactory international normative political theory through a critique and revision of orthodox views' while Hoffman, who vehemently criticizes Beitz's approach to this problem, nevertheless contends that 'the advantage of imperatives is that they provide at least a sense of direction' (Beitz, 1979: vii; Hoffman, 1981: 57f, 43). And Michael Doyle, too, holds that Realists overlook certain political achievements, as, for instance, the peace that stable democratic states have been able to keep between themselves. For this fact suggests, argues Doyle, not only that the relations between liberal states 'differ from the state of war' which Realists assume to be the normal condition of the international, but also that the relations between liberal and non-liberal states differ from 'the prudent, strategic calculation that Realists hope will inform the foreign policies of states in an insecure world' (Doyle, 1983: 235). In other words, there are areas of potential moral consideration and action in theory as well as in practice, which Realists overlook.

Is it the case, then, that Liberals do not perceive the diversity of cultures as a fundamental problem of international relations? Stanley Hoffman, who is very close to the Realists in this respect, holds that the domestic sphere is governed by a conception of justice whereas order in the international sphere is in constant flux (1981: 19). This is so because in the latter we do not find a 'single, operational international code of behavior. There are competing codes, rival philosophical traditions, clashing conceptions of morality' (Hoffman, 1981: 19). Not only, says Hoffman, is there no 'single moral code' in the international sphere but there are also 'no effective substitutes' (1981: 20). Neither international law, nor international organizations nor world public opinion make up for this lack of cultural unity. Indeed, international law, organizations and world public opinion are limited in their effectiveness by precisely this cultural diversity, by the different value systems, norms, and governmental institutions erected on their basis. This does not mean, according to Hoffman, that the clash of values and belief systems automatically translates into clashes among states, that there can be no peaceful co-existence between different value systems or that war between states is always to be understood as a clash between cultures. But rival value systems do very frequently bring the international 'very close to the pole of enmity' (Hoffman, 1981: 20). For Hoffman the basic problem of the international, that which distinguishes the international from the domestic, is the absence of a common culture, of common conceptions of justice and morality. Although this does not mean that all international conflicts can be understood as struggles between cultures, ultimately, the very fact of the existence of different cultures, theoretically, distinguishes the international from the domestic.

Although posed in different terms, Doyle makes a similar statement. Taking the conditions of peace and war as his starting point, Doyle points out that liberal states have established a stable peace among themselves but have utterly failed in keeping peace with non-liberal states (1983: 213–15, 323). This, he argues, is significant for the conception of the international precisely because it undermines some of the Realist assumptions. It suggests, Doyle argues, that there is more to be known about the international than that it is made up of different states prudently calculating power relations and defending themselves, if need be pre-emptively, against other states. It suggests that the internal make-up of states plays a role for their behaviour in foreign policy. The difference between liberal and non-liberal states is not just a difference of power or wealth, which could be captured in the Realist framework, Doyle argues, but 'liberals are fundamentally different', that is qualitatively different (1983: 235). This qualitative difference is one of culture; for what unites liberal states and distinguishes them from non-liberal states is, according to Doyle, a set of values and institutions designed to realize those values. Among these values are 'the freedom of the individual', the 'rights of private property, including the owner-ship of means of production', and the right to 'democratic participation or representation' (Doyle, 1983: 206–8). Among the institutions designed to realize or guarantee those rights are a free press, equality under the law, elections, education and health care institutions open to all members of society and so on. What makes for the failure of the liberal states in keeping peace with non-liberal states is the fact that the latter do not adhere to the same, the liberal, values and do not establish the institutions which might promote and guarantee them. Therefore, holds Doyle, 'liberals do not merely distrust what they do; we dislike what they are – public violators of human rights', for instance in the case of the communist states (1983: 330). Liberal states, therefore, have often turned conflicts of interest between themselves and others into 'crusades'; they start campaigns for democracy, they intervene against 'enemies of free enterprise', they support free trade and investment, and human rights (1983: 324, 330, 334, 342). In short, the foreign policy of liberal states aims, according to Doyle, at the spread of liberal values and institutions in non-liberal states. Hence, the basis for many of the world's conflicts, for Doyle too, is the existence of different cultures, broadly distinguished as liberal and non-liberal.

Beitz's project of working out 'a cosmopolitan conception of inter-national morality is' explicitly 'not equivalent to, nor does it necessarily imply, a political program'; Beitz clearly distinguishes between 'moral structures' and 'political ones', and the bulk of his book deals with the former rather than the latter (1979: 182f). Notwithstanding this em-phasis, it is interesting to note that Beitz argues against 'the image of a global state of nature, in which nations are conceived as largely self-sufficient, purposive units' which

> has been thought to capture the relative absence of moral norms governing relations among states. At one extreme of the tradition – represented by Machiavelli, Bodin and Hobbes – international theory has denied the existence of any controlling universal rules in rela-tions between states, substituting *raison d'état* as the highest norm. Even when the possibility of international moral ties has been granted – for example, in post-Grotian writings on international law – these ties have been held to be substantially weaker than

intranational moral bonds precisely because of the absence of supra-national political authorities.

(1979: 3)

In contrast to these conceptions of the international as characterized by cultural diversity which makes universal morality either impossible or weak, Beitz wants to demonstrate that the international does, indeed, allow for or even demand a universal morality. But he does not argue that Realist conceptions of the international are and always have been wrong. In the past, he says, these conceptions might have been justified, but 'recent developments compel us to take another look' (1979: 3). What has changed in the world recently, according to Beitz, is an 'increasing sensitivity of domestic societies to external economic, polit-ical, and cultural events' (1979: 3). In other words, growing inter-dependence, increasing transnational interactions, that which today is commonly called globalization, has produced a world in which concep-tions of self-sufficient states as the basis for international theory are outdated, in which 'the image of a global state of nature no longer provides an obviously correct picture of the moral relations among states, persons of diverse nationality, and other actors in the interna-tional realm' (1979: 3f).[4] What Beitz attempts to show is that universal morality can, and has to be, grounded in individuals, not in states. Realist accounts accept, according to Beitz, the analogy between the individual and the state in the state of nature. And on the basis of that analogy, Realists invest states just like individual persons with rights. But, says Beitz, 'if the idea of the national interest plays any role in justifying prescriptions for state behavior, it can only be because the national interest derives its normative importance from these deeper and more ultimate concerns' (1979: 52f). Hence, in this view national survival, for instance, can only be accepted as a right if what it really means is the survival of the individual members of the nation; it cer-tainly is not a right for the survival of 'cultural life or to the defense of economic interests' (Beitz, 1979: 55). The right of self-determination, too, one of the cornerstones of modern international law, and singled out by Doyle and Hoffman as crucial for the preservation of at least a modicum of peace and order in the international system (Hoffman, 1981: 110; Doyle, 1983: 337, 344), is rejected by Beitz. It is not the case that Beitz rejects the idea of self-determination as such but, rather, he rejects the principle on which it is based, namely some important common characteristic – 'race, tribe, religion, or culture' (Beitz, 1979: 110f). And yet, in rejecting these arguments and attempting to derive rights from different principles, Beitz implies that the former are, indeed, operative in international politics, that, sadly, the acceptance of cultural difference as a given and as a source of rights is more the problem than the solution to international conflict and injustice. And, indeed, he states that the 'main difference between international relations and domestic society is the absence in the former case of effective decision-making and decision-enforcing institutions' and 'the absence of what might be called an international sense of community' (1979: 154f). Here, again, the international is defined as a culturally diverse realm, one in which the individual members do not develop a sense of community and do not, therefore, have the same 'motivational basis for compliance with laws' (1979: 155).

Just as in the case of the Realists one would expect that the Liberals would develop a theory of international relations at the heart of which we would find the problem of intercultural relations. But rather than culture, what we find again is nature. Liberal theories, too, are based on a conception of the state of nature. To be sure, Liberals reject vehemently the particular understanding of the state of nature the Realists emphasize, or are taken to emphasize, namely the state of nature as a state of war. Thus, Beitz rejects Hobbes's state of nature on two counts. Firstly, he argues that the analogy between Hobbes's state of nature as a state of war and contemporary international relations is empirically incorrect. For this conception presupposes that states are the actors in international relations, that they are relatively equal in power, that they are independent of each other with regard to their internal affairs and, finally, that between them there is no reliable expectation of reciprocity. Beitz holds 'that contemporary international relations does not meet any of these conditions' (1979: 36).

And, secondly, he argues that Hobbes's state of nature does not 'give a correct account of the justification of moral principles for the international realm' (Beitz, 1979: 35). For morality and moral rights ultimately reside with persons.

> When the state of nature is viewed as a moral construct, and interpreted as it is by Hobbes, it supplies an unacceptable account of the justification of moral principles ...; but even if Hobbes's metaethics were accepted, it is the interests of *persons* that are fundamental, and 'national interests' are relevant to the justification of international principles only to the extent that they are derived from the interests of persons.
>
> (Beitz, 1979: 64)

And this kind of argument, Beitz contends, has been made by Kant. 'Following Kant, we might call this a cosmopolitan conception. It is cosmopolitan in the sense that it is concerned with the moral relations of members of a universal community in which state boundaries have a merely derivative significance' (1979: 181f.). What Kant provides, and Hobbes does not, then, is an acceptable account of the justification of moral principles in individuals.

If this is, philosophically, an acceptable method of justifying moral principles, the question arises whether the implied continuity between individual members of a universal community and international relations holds. Beitz clearly thinks so.

> If the societies of the world are now to be conceived as open, fully interdependent systems, the world as a whole would fit the description of a scheme of social cooperation, and the arguments for the two principles[5] would apply, a fortiori, at the global level. The principles of justice for international politics would be the two principles for domestic society writ large.
>
> (1979: 132)

Beitz is convinced that 'international relations is coming more and more to resemble domestic relations' and, therefore, domestic principles of justice now can and have to be applied to the international (1979: 179).

If it is true that

> now national boundaries do not set off discrete, self-sufficient societies, we may not regard them as morally decisive features of the earth's social geography. For purposes of moral choice, we must, instead, regard the world from the perspective of an original position from which matters of national citizenship are excluded by an extended veil of ignorance.
>
> (1979: 176)

The state of nature, or original position, which is here suggested as the source of moral principles, domestic and international, is, indeed, not just stripped of national citizenship.

> Speaking very roughly, the moral point of view requires us to regard the world from the perspective of one person among many rather than from that of a particular self with particular interests, and to choose courses of action, policies, rules, and institutions on grounds

that would be acceptable to any agent who was impartial among the competing interests involved.

(1979: 58)

Indeed, what Beitz suggests here is that the problem of cultural diversity be solved by deriving universal normative principles from an original position or state of nature stripped of all cultural identities and particularities. In this original position or state of nature, human beings do, however, have one crucially important common characteristic, namely reason. Thus, Beitz, for instance, holds that real existing consent to government does not necessarily conform with universal morality and, therefore, he proposes a 'hypothetical contract' to solve the problem: that is, 'a government is legitimate if it *would be* consented to by rational persons subject to its rule' (1979: 80). Similarly, 'the test of a principle's neutrality is whether reasonable persons would endorse it...' (1979: 88). And it is this state of nature, this original position, provided through the Rawlsian veil of ignorance, which will enable us to work out the appropriate principles of justice, of distribution, of universal morality (Beitz, 1979: 141). Hence, just as in the case of Realism, we end up with a Liberal theory of International Relations based on a state of nature, which is characterized through an absence of culture and a presence of reason and, finally, in which reason becomes identified with morality (1979: 19).

Doyle, too, chooses Kant instead of Hobbes. But for Doyle, Kant's moral principle of treating individuals as ends rather than means enters the theory of International Relations in a different way. Unlike Beitz, Doyle concludes that 'the basic postulate of liberal international theory holds that states have the right to be free from foreign intervention. Since morally autonomous citizens hold rights to liberty, the states that democratically represent them have the right to exercise political independence' (Doyle, 1983: 213). Doyle follows Kant's exposition in the *Perpetual Peace* and argues that, ideally, the freedom of the individual in the state of nature leads to, or ought to lead to, the establishment of republican states. Because the latter are the product of the realization of the former's rights, they too have the right to independence. These republican states, in turn, freely enter into a pacific union. Doyle identifies the peace which liberal states have kept among themselves for 'almost 200 years' with this pacific union (1983: 217). But why have liberal states failed to keep the peace with non-liberal states? There are, according to Doyle, two reasons. 'First, outside the pacific union, liberal regimes, like all other states, are caught in the international state of war

Hobbes and the Realists describe' (1983: 324). Thus, individuals have left the state of nature when they set up republican regimes, but where these particular kinds of regime do not prevail, the state of nature in a Hobbesian sense, still reigns free. And this, then, is the second reason for the failure of liberal states to keep peace outside the pacific union. For they do not, according to their own principles, consider outsiders, non-liberals, as eligible to the same rights and obligations. 'According to liberal practice, some nonliberal states, such as the United States' communist rivals, do not acquire the right to be free from foreign intervention, nor are they assumed to respect the political independence and territorial integrity of other states' (1983: 325).

For Doyle, the international is defined by the clash of two different kinds of nature. Liberal regimes are considered – by their own supporters, that is – as legitimate because they are erected on the principle of the 'natural' liberty of individuals. The relationship between liberal and non-liberal states is to be understood as one of the state of nature in the Hobbesian sense, the state of war. At the end of the article, Doyle returns to Kant's understanding of 'nature'. For in Kant's theory it is 'nature's secret design' which will eventually lead to peace. Nature has made human beings settle all over the globe, and since in different climates and locations nature provides human beings with different resources, people start to trade and exchange. This is the 'transnational' path to peace 'through the ties of trade, cultural exchange, and political understanding that together both commit existing republics to peace and, by inference, give rise to individualistic demands in nonrepublics whose resolution requires the establishment of republican government' (Doyle, 1983: 351). It is the same nature which made people settle all over the globe, however, which put quite considerable distances between them that are in turn responsible for the development of different cultures, different religions and different languages. These, then, give rise to the second path towards peace which 'operates through the pressure of insecurity and of actual war that together engender republican governments – the domestic constitutional foundations for peace' (1983: 351). Doyle suggests that Kant might have been right, that the past development towards peace and republicanism was actually triggered by these two dynamics, both of which are derived from nature.

Hoffman, too, starts out with a critique (and vindication) of the Hobbesian state of nature as a state of war. He points out that it is, of course, empirically not true that international relations are a state of war; and it is also not true that the goal of political action in the international sphere must, by definition, always be security and survival (Hoffman, 1981: 14). However, he does accept that the international system is structured in such a way that the 'moral opportunities for the statesman in world affairs are quite limited' (1981: 19). In describing this difference, in moral terms, between the domestic and the international, Hoffman constructs a hierarchy of moralities in the social order. At the bottom of this hierarchy we find individual morality either in its religious – for instance, Christian – or in its philosophic, Kantian variety. At the next level, there are various group moralities clearly characterized by diminished altruism. And at the top we find the statesman who adheres to a different code of morality dictated by the good of the country (1981: 23).

And, argues Hoffman, the range of moral choices a statesman has, depends quite considerably on the structure of the society in which he operates. Thus, an ethical foreign policy has to aim at transforming the 'the international arena from the state of a jungle to that of a society' in order to widen the moral choices statesmen have (1981: 35f). And at this point, Hoffman remarks, 'we have gone back to Kant in two ways. First of all, he was not wrong to believe that if one wants to move in that direction, one prerequisite is domestic: what he called the constitutional governments' (1981: 36). Thus, the establishment of republican or constitutional governments is a major stepping stone towards international peace and morality. And if Hoffman is not very far from Doyle in this respect, he comes even closer with the second way in which Kant seems to be important. For, just like Doyle, he considers the present international system as one in which the danger of nuclear war on the one hand and social and economic interdependence on the other forces states to cooperate if for no other reason but in order to ensure their pure survival (1981: 37). And survival and interdependence, war and trade, are, of course, 'nature's secret design'.

Hoffman accepts to quite a great extent the structural limitations for morality in the international sphere as it exists and, thus, comes quite close to the Realists. But he does believe that an ought is also necessary; in fact, he defines Liberalism as the belief in a '(limited and reversible) perfectibility of man and society, and particularly in the possibility of devising institutions, based on consent, that will make society more humane and more just, and the citizen's lot better' (1981: 8). And it is because he believes that questions about morality are ultimately grounded in individuals that he concentrates on the moral decisions that individuals, statesmen, have to make in the international sphere. Although groups are important and the moral notions of individuals are very much shaped within the framework of groups, Hoffman gives the statesman a chance for moral development which is not restricted to groups (1981: 9). He argues that abstract notions of morality, irrespective of the realities of the world, are at best useless and at worst dangerous (1981: 26f.). What he proposes, then, is a realistic account of how the world is and what is possible within that framework, and then he adds to this the moral imperatives which are to give direction to human striving for a better world. That is, the world is made up of a plurality of cultures none of which can claim a monopoly in truth or morality; this recognition, however, does not relieve us from making moral decisions and defending our own value system against those 'practices and policies that violate our notion of humanity' (1981: 37f.).

This notion of humanity includes a number of fundamental rights for human beings, Hoffman argues, 'that derive from their nature as living, feeling, and thinking beings' (1981: 109f). Hoffman's solution to the problem of morality in international affairs, then, turns out to be a combination of two kinds of 'nature': the 'nature' of international politics as it is, and the 'nature' of the individual human being. The former demands a great degree of tolerance for diverse values and cultures including the preservation of the independence of states and balance of power politics while the latter dictates respect for human rights and distributive justice (1981: 189f).

This exposition of the considerable common ground that Realist and Liberal International Relations theories share explains the commonalities between Samuel Huntington and Francis Fukuyama mentioned in the beginning of this chapter. Both Liberals and Realists distinguish the domestic from the international with reference to the cultural diversity of the latter and the relative cultural homogeneity of the former. To be sure, Realists do stress the absence or presence of government as a distinguishing feature between the domestic and the international but, as discussed, government itself is seen by all of them as derived from, and only possible in, a culturally relatively homogeneous society. The absence of government in the international sphere, ultimately, is due to the fact that the world's population is culturally heterogeneous. And if Liberals accuse Realists of reifying the state they overlook the very basis the state rests on in Realist thought. Simultaneously, however, this critique of Realism allows Liberals to emphasize individuals as the source and end of international politics over and against the state and to downplay the fact that at least certain kinds of states do have just as inviolable rights for the Liberals as for the Realists: liberal states, states which can claim to uphold certain natural rights of individuals. The international sphere is for both theories characterized by cultural diversity, only for the Realists every state as such represents a particular culture, while for the Liberals the world is generally divided into states with a liberal culture and states representing non-liberal cultures.

Both theories also share a particular approach to solving this problem of cultural diversity, for both turn to nature as something universal, something common to all of humanity. The universality of nature, however, plays a twofold role. On the one hand, it represents the possibility of making general statements about the world, about international politics, irrespective of the cultural particularities it is made up of. On the other hand, and more importantly, universal human nature is defined by reason which, in turn, opens up the possibility of overcoming the particular cultural identities and interests and with them, of course, the conflicts they generate in the international sphere. And, thus, reason as an integral part of human nature is not only defined as the opposite of culture but also identified with morality. If cultural diversity produces clashing moralities, reason will, it is hoped, be the basis for one universal morality, either of the statesmen or of the individuals. Thus, culture is the problem and nature the solution.

There is a third element, though, which Realist and Liberal theories of International Relations have in common. They both argue from the domestic to the international. Both take domestic communities and their respective cultures, interests, moralities as given and then construct the international sphere and its structures on the basis of those domestic givens. There is, indeed, always implied the hierarchy of moralities Hoffman described, starting with individual morality, moving on to group and state moralities and, eventually, a rather weak international morality.

But if it was possible, thus far, to demonstrate that culture is conceived as the problem of the international and nature as the solution, this does not yet tell us where this idea of nature as opposed to culture comes from and what its specific meaning is. Hence, in the following pages I will trace the origin of this concept of the state of nature back to its roots in the international encounter between Spaniards and Amerindians in the course of the discovery of America. In the course of this exposition it will also become clear that moral and cultural development is not just a one-way street . . . that, indeed, the Western concept of the state of nature has its origins in an international encounter.

Part I

Historical Origins of the State of Nature

2
The 'Discovery' of America as a Culture Shock

'In our days', wrote Montesquieu in *The Spirit of the Laws*, 'we receive three different or contrary educations, namely, of our parents, of our masters, and of the world. What we learn in the latter effaces all the ideas of the former' (1949: 33). This world, or rather that part of the world which Montesquieu would still 200 years later experience as contradicting all the teachings of parents and masters, was 'discovered' by the Spaniards in 1492. This 'discovery' triggered a unique and crucial debate among the Spaniards at the time. It was unique because it was the only case in which a European power accompanied the process of colonization with an officially sponsored public debate about its legitimacy. And it was of crucial importance because it was in the course of this debate that Spanish discussants developed the concept of the state of nature in its modern sense, a concept which subsequently came to underpin European political thought, in both its domestic and international varieties – in fact, eventually the concept revolutionized all branches of the sciences but, in particular, the social sciences (Parry, 1981: 15f; Meek, 1976: 3).

The Spanish discussants I am going to concentrate on are Bartolemé de Las Casas, Juan Ginés de Sepúlveda, and Francisco de Vitoria. Las Casas had originally come to America with the *conquistadores* and had himself been granted Amerindian workers for his *encomienda* (land entitlement). Under the influence of the passionate sermons of the Dominican Montesinos against the ill-treatment of the Amerindians by Spanish *encomenderos*, Las Casas entered the Dominican Order and fought for the rest of his life for the rights of the Amerindians. In the course of his campaining, he continuously travelled back and forth between America and Spain where he made presentations to the Court which, eventually, declared him officially Protector of the Indians. Las

Casas wrote profusely on Spanish–Amerindian relations and defended the freedom of the Amerindians before the *junta*, the council, discussing their legal status in Valladolid in 1550/51. His opponent in front of that *junta* was Juan Ginés de Sepúlveda. Sepúlveda was an Aristotle scholar who had never been to America and relied for his information on the extremely biased writings of the official Crown historian for America, Gonzalo Fernández de Oviedo y Valdés. Sepúlveda argued that the Amerindians were natural slaves as defined by Aristotle and could, therefore, be legally enslaved by the Spaniards. The third writer, Francisco de Vitoria, was Professor at the University of Salamanca and, in 1537/38, gave lectures on the legal status of the Amerindians and the rights of the Spanish Crown in America. His lectures on this topic treat the subject very systematically. Indeed, it is on the basis of these lectures that Vitoria is held by some contemporary scholars to be the 'founder' of modern international law.

But before the debate itself can be analysed, it has to be established why the 'discovery' of America should have triggered a debate in the first place. This is curious because the debate itself revolved around three concrete issues, namely whether the Spaniards had a right to establish their rule in America, whether they could lead just wars against the Amerindians, and whether they had the right to enslave the latter (Pagden, 1982: 32, 37, 1993: 52; Hanke, 1974: 40, 125; Dickason, 1988: 54ff; Sánchez, 1994: 216f). And all these activities – conquest or rule, war, and slavery – were not only common in Europe before the 'discovery' of America but there also existed a wide body of legal rules on these issues. Why, then, did the Spaniards not simply apply the existing rules to the Amerindians? It could not just have been the fact that America and its people were an unexpected discovery for, after all, the contemporary European 'knowledge' of the world not only allowed for, but even expected, the possibility of all kinds of wonderful and miraculous islands, peoples, monsters and animals to be 'discovered'. It could also not just have been the cultural difference between Spaniards and Amerindians, for in this case one would expect the Portuguese explorations of the Western coast of Africa to have triggered such a debate. Similarly, European interaction with non-European and non-Christian peoples was by no means a new phenomenon. And the particular interests the Spaniards pursued in America – to subdue the native population by military means, to erect their own rule and to command the labour of the indigenous peoples – had been a common feature of European military expeditions throughout the Middle Ages. Why was there no debate about the missionary expeditions of the militant orders into the

Baltic region? The reason why the Spaniards had to have that debate, as I will set out in this chapter, was not that the Amerindians were pagans; it was not that they were considered 'savages' or 'barbarians'; and it was not a lack of experience or legal justification with conquest and slavery. It was, rather, that the existence of America and the Amerindian peoples defied the *cultural meaning* of the world – established through European historical experiences and interpreted through the prism of the Christian faith.

Apart from Europe, Asia and Africa were 'known' to Europeans at the time. And this 'knowledge' was based on a mix of eyewitness accounts from Marco Polo's *Travels* through the fantastic tales of Sir John Mandeville to the *Historia Rerum Ubique Gestarum* by Pope Pius II, Pliny's *Natural History* and Plutarch's *Lives*, not to mention the Bible, popular legends, and sea stories relating tales of foreign lands abounding in gold and silver, rivers of pearls, precious jewels, spices, unguents, mythical animals, cannibals, giants, Amazons, monsters, the rich and powerful legendary Christian kingdom of Prester John, the ten lost tribes of Israel, the paradise island of St Brendan, the terrestrial paradise and other wondrous things (Flint, 1992: 16, 39, 53–77; Scammell, 1992: 57). All these marvels were systematically depicted on medieval maps. Among the very popular authors who provided the template for the abundance of monstrous races were Pliny, Solinus and Isidore. The home of most of these wonders was India, the Indies or Asia (Flint, 1992: 16, 39). These were the maps which the Portuguese used in their early explorations of the African coast, hoping to find not just the source of the gold which appeared on the Moroccan markets but also the Christian kingdom of Prester John who might assist them financially and militarily in their struggle against the pernicious but powerful forces of the infidel Muslims (Parry, 1981: 35; Leed, 1995: 13; Scammell, 1992: 57). And these were the maps which Cristóbal Colón used to find his way across the Atlantic heading for the riches and marvels of the lands of the Great Khan (China) which were supposed to assist the Spanish Crown in fitting out the last crusade against the indidels before the end of the world (Todorov, 1999: 9–12; Flint, 1992: 197–202; Scammell, 1992: 58).

When Colón set out to sail west, the eyewitness accounts of Asia were outdated. They had been written at the end of the thirteenth and the beginning of the fourteenth centuries when the Mongols 'tolerant in religion, desirous of trade, curious about the world outside' made travel safe (Parry, 1981: 6). These travels were subsequently made impossible by the Black Death devastating most of Europe and Asia, by the

Ottoman Turks who converted to Islam and fought against Christendom, and by the Chinese successors to Mongol rule in China who were much more inward looking and much less interested in interaction with the 'barbarians' from the West (Parry, 1981: 7). But the Europeans of the late Middle Ages were altogether incapable of distinguishing between the authenticity of an eyewitness account of China, like Marco Polo's, and the fantastic tales of Sir John Mandeville (Parry, 1981: 8). It was this impossibility of disentangling 'correct' knowledge, outdated knowledge and pure fantasy which made the search for Prester John as serious an undertaking as the goal of reaching the Mongol Court in China long after the Ming dynasty had taken over (Scammell, 1992: 57f; Leed, 1995: 13). Yet, it was not just the case that Europeans *could* not distinguish between empirical geographical and anthropological knowledge and fantasies but rather that they *would* not do so. In order to draw up these maps, the mapmakers used as much material as they could lay their hands on – starting with the Bible, through histories, encyclopedias and legends. In order to be considered authentic the material had to meet two requirements: the first was, of course, that it had to be in conformity with the teachings of the Bible, and secondly the works had to 'actively assist in that attitude of wondering amazement which God's work of creation must never cease to inspire in true Christians' (Flint, 1992: 15). These medieval maps, then, were not so much exercises in geography but means of moral and religious education, polemics against heresy, and proselytizing material (Flint, 1992: 7). What counted as *true* knowledge was governed by religious beliefs, and knowledge was produced and extended by reading and rereading, interpreting and reinterpreting, the canon of authoritative ancient and Christian authors (Parry, 1981: 10; Pagden, 1993: 52).

Knowledge about the world, then, was not neutral information; rather, knowledge always had a purpose, a religious purpose – it played a role in God's design for the world and human beings in it. Hence, the three continents shown on these *mappae mundi* – Asia, Europe and Africa – were, according to the Bible, the dry lands given by God to the three sons of Noah: Asia was the domain of Shem, Europe that of Japhet and Africa that of Ham. Jerusalem and the Mediterranean were located in the centre (Flint, 1992: 9). All men, according to the Bible, had descended from Adam through the three sons of Noah, and all of them had been preached the Christian faith by the apostles. Accordingly, there could not be any other inhabited part of the world than those three continents. To be sure, there were stories and legends about as yet unknown islands in the Atlantic – the legendary Atlantis being only one of them – and it was also physically possible that there were landmasses on the back of the globe. However, it was impossible that human beings could live there or even reach them because that would have contradicted the teachings of the Bible (Flint, 1992: 33; Parry, 1981: 148). Hence, for the Europeans at the time it was perfectly natural to believe in the existence and discovery of dog-headed people, Amazons and the like – all of which were depicted on the authoritative medieval maps – but perfectly impossible to believe in the existence of an inhabited continent 'on the back of the globe'. This, then, is the first difference between, say, Portuguese explorations in Africa and the Spanish 'discovery' of America. The existence of Africa was part and parcel of the medieval world view, and even if the Portuguese had found the most incredible monsters there, these, too, would have been taken for granted.

But, even so, if the practical goals the Spaniards pursued in America were no different from those pursued in other contexts, why should it have proven so difficult to simply extend the pre-existing political practices and legal justifications to the Amerindians? The two overwhelming motivations for the early explorations were the pursuit of wealth justified by, and in the service of, the spread of the Christian faith (Scammell, 1992: 59; Parry, 1981: 19). The relationship between these two goals is quite an entangled and complicated one in its domestic European as well as in its international dimension. In comparison with the greater part of the known world, in the fifteenth century Europe was ravaged by wars, by epidemic diseases, by famines, by the sharpest social inequalities including slavery, and by witch hunts, various forms of brutality and chaos in the cities (Stannard, 1992: 57–62). In short, Europe was poor and backward. To be sure, a tiny minority in European society was rich and so was the Church. But for the overwhelming majority of the European population life expectancy was very low, and infant mortality rates were astronomically high (1992: 60f). Europeans did not have any delusions about their standard of civilization in comparison with most of the rest of the world known to them. Concepts of barbarism and civilization were well known from ancient authors like Aristotle, Herodotus and Tacitus. For the ancient Romans, the home of civilization had been in the South, around the Mediterranean, and barbarians lived north of the Alps. And this was still the going distinction in Renaissance Italy (Wolff, 1994: 4f). In historical perspective, then, medieval Europeans were convinced that the ancient Greeks and Romans had been much more civilized and better informed than they themselves were. In comparison with the rest of the contemporary world, they considered, and for some time to come, the Far East, China and Japan, India and even the bitterly resented Islamic world as superior civilizations (Parry, 1981: 9; Bitterli, 1982: 52, 55, 59–63; Leed, 1995: 111, 113). Although all these other civilizations were believed to be deeply misguided with respect to revealed religion, Europeans nevertheless acknowledged that they had received most of the ancient writings through the Muslims, that they were dependent for their 'knowledge' about Africa almost entirely on Muslim and Jewish sources, and before the reign of Ferdinand and Isabella, the Spaniards admired and imitated Muslim civilization, customs and crafts at all levels of society, including the Court (Parry, 1990: 29, 1981: 5f). This judgement on the level of European civilization was shared by others: in India, the Portuguese and their European goods were considered dirty, crude and uncivilized and would never have been able to gain any ground in open competition with the Arab traders, while the Chinese and Japanese had no doubts that the Europeans they came into contact with were barbarians (Bitterli, 1982: 66f; Parry, 1981: 143).

In the centuries before the discovery of America, poverty and acute social inequality had given rise to two kinds of development in Europe. On the one hand, people attempted desperately to acquire wealth and social standing. The main sources of wealth at the time were land and command of the labour to work it. Trade was another, but much less attractive, way of bettering one's condition. There were essentially three drawbacks to the possibilities of trade. First of all, trade was 'replete with opportunities for every kind of sin' like 'bartering... worthless objects for precious ones,... price-rigging, short-changing, false weighing, fraudulent quality control..., connivance with thieves, insider-trading, excessive profit, trading on feast days, lying in the making of marriage contracts and, of course, usury' (Flint, 1992: 200). The worst of all of them, however, was to conduct trade with the Turkish Sultan without papal licence. And since most trade in luxury goods – the trade which really payed – was with the East and, therefore, involved cooperation with the Muslims, this was not an avenue open to a Christian knight who might be allowed to trade with other Christians but under no circumstances with infidels (Flint, 1992: 200; Parry, 1981: 35). Secondly, trade had to be financed up front and the returns were in no way certain; it was a risky business. And, thirdly, the trade in luxury goods was almost entirely in the hands of the Venetians and Genoese and, therefore, provided no great opportunities for the rest of Europe (Parry, 1981: 19f). With trade in the direct sense of the term more or less out of the question, the Europeans could, and did, revert to a very traditional way of bettering their condition. They embarked on military expeditions which might provide them with the opportunity to plunder, to bring land and people under their control whose religion, or lack thereof, might be used to justify outright conquest and colonization. These kinds of expedition could also be used to disrupt or prey on the infidel trade which might be construed as a form of indirect crusade depriving the enemy of the means of waging war against Christianity (Parry, 1981: 21, 35).

Historically, military expeditions for the purpose of acquiring wealth had been a common feature in many societies. The ancient Greeks as well as the Vikings organized military expeditions for this purpose regularly as joint stock ventures, just as did later on the East India Company and others of the kind (Leed, 1995: 42f). Quite frequently, too, the profit to be made would not be as much in the plunder of material wealth, of which there was not always that much to be found, but in taking human captives whose labour could be exploited and the command over whom would immediately raise the social status of the conqueror (1995: 44f, 55). This was the kind of activity the Europeans were engaged in in those small pockets at the margins of Western Christianity which were considered even more uncivilized than Europe itself was: in the Baltic region, in Ireland, in the Canaries. The only difference between the traditional and the Christian conquering and colonizing expeditions was that the latter demanded of their victims the conversion to Christianity. This was the case with the crusades to the Baltic region where the Church gave a title to the colonizing orders justifying these undertakings as missionary activities (1995: 77). This was also the situation in the Canaries where the indigenous Guanches resisted the Christianizing and 'civilizing' efforts of the Spaniards with such a vengeance that their colonization could not be completed until well after the discovery of America and the establishment of the India trade (Parry, 1990: 40–2). The English, who had set their eyes on Ireland, had to argue that the Irish, although they were Christians, did not live like proper Christians but conducted their social life in an entirely uncivilized way. On the basis of this argument at the height of the crusading era, they managed to get a title to 'civilize' Ireland from the only ever English Pope, Adrian IV (Williams, 1992: 136f). 'Protection of life and property was guaranteed only to those of the Irish who spoke and lived like English people' (1992: 137). Throughout the Middle Ages, then, European poverty and backwardness had led to wars, slavery and the extension of European or Christian rule over other peoples for the purpose of acquiring wealth. And nothing more or less than that was the goal of the Spaniards in America just as the political practices to achieve this end in no way differed from the ones frequently employed in Europe. The difference between the 'barbarians' encountered in the Baltic region, in Ireland or in the Canaries and those encountered in America was, again, that the former were 'known' to Europeans while the latter were not even supposed to exist.

Another, the second, development which took shape in Europe as a consequence of the 'notorious affluence of the church and the pursuit of benefices by ambitious worldly careerists' was a reform movement within and outside the Church (Aston, 1968: 152). Within the Church this movement attempted to purify the clergy by laying renewed stress on vows of poverty. It preached an austere Christianity and demanded of the clergy that they go out and work among the poor peasants. It was particularly strong in the Franciscan order but had, at the end of the fifteenth century, also gained ground with the Dominicans and Jeronymites. It sympathized with reformers like Erasmus and was later, in the sixteenth century, accused of Lutheranism (Parry, 1981: 29f). A rethinking of the relationship between wealth and religion, however, did not only take place within the Church. Indeed, if asceticism originally had been the way of life in monasteries and was not expected to be practised by lay Christians, it now became drawn into secular society and lay at the heart of a movement of puritanism which combined worldly activity with a pious life (Aston, 1968: 149, 172f). In Spain this new combination was also fed by Renaissance literary conventions and the experiences of the *reconquista*, as a result of which Spaniards developed a cult of the individual and a 'passion for personal reputation' (Parry, 1981: 31). In Franciscan teaching, the pursuit of wealth as such was singled out as particularly sinful. There were, however, mitigating circumstances. One possibility was to take great risks and to put one's life at stake in the pursuit of wealth – and this is what the early explorers and *conquistadores* practised to excess. They endured – of their own free will, to be sure – extreme hardships and most of them died a violent death (Parry, 1990: 98; Leed, 1995: 44–6). Yet, the most important and effective honest outlet the Franciscans devised for the sin of material acquisitiveness was to put wealth into the service of religion, in particular in the service of the Christian mission (Flint, 1992: 192). The pursuit of wealth and religious beliefs, thus, were deeply interwoven for fifteenth century Europeans.

But when we think back to the medieval *mappae mundi* and to the practical interaction of Christendom with outsiders, it is clear that the real pull of wealth would not be exerted by those small pockets of 'poverty' and 'backwardness' at the outer margins of Western Christianity – in the Baltic, Ireland, the Canaries. The area which truly triggered the imagination of the Europeans was the East. It was in the East that all the objects of European desires, material and religious, were to be found. That was where a great number of superior civilizations were flourishing; that was where all the riches came from; that was where Europeans believed to be the home of all kinds of marvellous and wondrous things; and that was where legends located either other Christian kingdoms as potential allies against Islam, or pagans who were so reasonable that they would take on the teachings of Christianity without any resistance (Leed, 1995: 102). At the time of the early explorations, however, the East and all its riches and miracles were inaccessible to Europeans. The powerful Muslims controlled the trade and fought Christendom, not just in the Middle East but also in Northern Africa. The political relations with the Muslim world had for centuries taken the form of a power struggle, on both sides justified by religious zeal. Towards the end of the fifteenth century the overwhelming military power of the Muslims was generally acknowledged. Despite the fact that the language of the crusading spirit was very much alive, European rulers did not actually believe that a traditional crusade would have any chance of success. Next to their civilizational and military superiority, Europeans by this time had also had to accept that the Muslims were not only proud and extremely loyal and intellectually capable defenders of their religion but also very successful prosyletizers, as the rapid conversion of the Ottoman tribes clearly demonstrated. The conversion of Muslims by way of preaching and rational disputation was, thus, not a viable alternative either (Parry, 1981: 25). Within Europe, the only exception was found on the Iberian Peninsula, where the idea of the crusade still had a lot of currency in the fifteenth century. This is, of course, not surprising, in light of the fact that the *reconquista* was the only success story against Islam at the time, which had just brought the whole peninsula back under Christian rule. In addition, the closeness of the North African coast in Muslim hands presented a constant threat to the Christian integrity of Spain and Portugal.

The problem the Iberian rulers faced, then, was twofold. On the one hand, the close proximity of the powerful and well organized Muslims in North Africa motivated them to go on fighting; on the other hand the very same power and previous losses made it difficult to convince other Christian rulers to support these extremely expensive undertakings. The early explorations of the Portuguese and Spaniards were, thus, motivated by the attempt to gain wealth as the necessary means for another successful crusade. Prince Henry of Portugal, the 'Navigator', for instance, supported early Portuguese explorations. They were intended to find the countries from which the gold that appeared on Moroccan markets came and the legendary Christian kingdom of Prester John with whom the Portuguese could not only engage in profitable trade but who might also become an ally in the crusade against the infidel Muslims. If these objectives could not be achieved, the Portuguese could still prey on and interrupt the trade of the infidels and, thus, deprive them of their means of making war against Christianity (Parry, 1981: 21, 35). Prince Henry was, quite in line with the general medieval mood, obsessed with crusades and

> reconciled himself only late in his career, and then reluctantly, to the trade which his captains initiated – for lack of Christian princes in Africa – with pagan peoples. He was always ready to drop the indirect crusade of the African voyage in favour of direct military assaults upon Morocco, whenever his royal relatives could be persuaded to mount these costly and fruitless adventures.
>
> (Parry, 1981: 36)

The Portuguese explorations along the Western coast of Africa did not, however, confront them with the same problems the Spaniards faced in America. Apart from the fact that the continent of Africa had always been an integral part of the European worldview, the Portuguese found long stretches of the African coast inaccessible for their ships. Their encounter with Africa and Africans was consequently reduced to those few areas where their ships could land. And what they found there often bore no great surprises for them. At the mouth of the Senegal and Gambia rivers, for instance, they, once again, found that the Muslims had arrived before them and organized society along the conventional lines; at the coast of what is now Ghana they were able to trade gold; and at the mouth of the Benin river they encountered the slave and pepper traders of the powerful and highly developed kingdom of Benin (Parry, 1981: 132f.). In fact, for a long time to come, Europeans did not know anything about the interior of Asia and Africa. In Asia, their knowledge was restricted to the great trading routes which any traveller would use. Apart from that, theirs was a knowledge of coastlines and trading stations (1981: 321f.).

For the Spaniards the general motivation for the early explorations and their desire to carry on with the crusades was the same as for the Portuguese. The predominance of religion over the desire for wealth was even more prominent in Spain where Isabella, the 'Catholic', after bring-ing the whole of the peninsula back under Christian rule did not follow the example of her predecessors and allow Muslims and Jews to live as vassals under Christian overlordship. As peaceful preaching and persua-sion proved unsuccessful in converting Muslims and Jews to Christian-ity, she embarked on violent baptism of the Muslims and expulsion of the Jews (Parry, 1981: 29). But in Isabella's dealing with the Jewish and Muslim populations in Spain she had, just like Prince Henry of Portugal, given priority to the religious desire of conversion over the material wealth she could have extracted from her non-Christian subjects had she followed the established practice of extracting special taxes from them.

With wars, crusades, slavery and the extension of rule over other peoples having been such common features of medieval politics, it does not come as a surprise that Europe had well-developed theories justifying these practices. And since there was nothing particularly new in either the goal of the Spaniards in America or in the means of achieving this goal, at first sight it seems inexplicable that the Spaniards could not just use those legal theories and apply them to the Amerin-dians. And yet, the legal theories of the Europeans were just as much based on the religious worldview as was geographical knowledge. In particular, it was a religious understanding of the history and destiny of humankind which, in the last instance, provided the basis for the legal justification of government, war and slavery. Originally, for Chris-tians true human nature had only existed before the Fall when human beings 'enjoyed liberty, equality, and the common use of all goods. Government, involving the subjection of man to man, like the institu-tions of slavery and property, was a divinely sanctioned remedy and punishment for sin' (Canning, 1996: 40). Human beings in this original state of innocence were clearly social beings and the hierarchical order of the family – the subordination of women and children to men – was thought to be natural; but political subordination was not (1996: 40). By the time of the discovery of America, however, the reading of Aristotle had complicated things, for Aristotle argued that human beings were by nature political beings. While for the pre-Aristotelian Christian approach human beings could certainly not fulfil their destiny within the *polis*, Aristotelian ideas opened up the possibility of an independent, secular political dimension of human life (1996: 127f). Within Europe the debate about the proper relationship between spiritual and temporal rule, between the papacy and worldly rulers, had, in fact, gone on for a long time (1996: 114–34; Pagden, 1990: 14). This debate, however, also had 'international' implications. For if, as one school of thought argued, *extra ecclesiam non est imperium,* infidel rule would always be unjust, it could exist only *de facto* but never *de jure.* This line of thinking accredited to the Pope the right to dispose of the lands of infidels as he saw fit. The other position distinguished between worldly and spiritual power. Here it was argued that because human beings are by nature political beings, political communities were natural communities, subject to natural law rather than divine law. If this was the case, then political communities did not necessarily have to be Christian in order to be recognized (Dickason, 1988: 54ff).

There was agreement, however, that Christian territory could never come justly under infidel rule. And any territory which at any point in time had either had a Christian population or a Christian ruler, no matter how this situation had come about and for how long it had lasted, was considered inalienable Christian territory. Essentially, the whole of the former Roman Empire was thus defined as inalienable Christian territory. Wars against Muslims, then, were generally justified on the grounds that they had conquered Christian territory (Vitoria, 1991: 289; Las Casas, 1971a: 8). The crusades to recapture Jerusalem were indeed neither conducted nor justified as missionary enterprises. Their purpose was not the mass conversion of Muslims but rather the *reconquest* of what was considered inalienable Christian territory with Jerusalem at the heart of it. They were a kind of armed pilgrimage (Leed, 1995: 68, 73f). This is not to say, of course, that material interests did not play a role in them. The crusades provided an outlet for the uprooted and starving masses in European societies which turned to 'murder and devour one another', as Pope Urban II put it; this incentive for the crusades, to externalize the internal war and misery by leading the superfluous population to the land of 'milk and honey', has been acknowledged throughout the period by Europeans themselves (cf. Leed, 1995: 67f). These plunders, rapes and massacres of the crusading armies were only missionary 'in the sense that the Church sanctified, directed, and organized the violence of a European soldiery, giving them an unambiguously Christian identity' (Leed, 1995: 74).

This argument, that infidels had unjustly conquered inalienable Christian territory, could not be made about crusades to the Baltic region, Ireland or the Canaries, and it could not be made about heretics and Jews, whose persecution within European societies was also depicted as a just war. The argument with respect to these people was that since according to the Bible the Christian religion had been preached to all peoples, those who despite their knowledge of the true religion stubbornly refused to become Christians were a hindrance to the spread of the Christian faith and, thus, enemies of it (Las Casas, 1971a: 8). And, indeed, if the military expeditions into the countries of these peoples were combined with missionary activity, then one could relatively easily produce a situation in which the establishment of Christian rule would be justified. For, if either a pagan ruler or the majority of a pagan population converted to Christianity, Christian rule could be established even against the will of the people (Vitoria, 1991: 287ff.). Vitoria clearly agreed with Las Casas that

> it would be harsh to deny them, who have never done us any wrong, the rights we concede to Saracens and Jews, who have been continual enemies of the Christian religion. Yet we do not deny the right of ownership of the latter, unless it be in the case of Christian lands which they have conquered.
>
> (Vitoria, 1991: 250f)

The difference between the Amerindians and any other people the Spaniards knew was simply that the Amerindians were neither Christians nor could they be accused of being enemies of Christianity – enemies in the sense of having known the true religion and resisting it. In addition, since they could not be accused of having conquered Christian territory, the Spaniards simply had no legal category with which to capture the Amerindians. Before the discovery of America, in legal terms based on the Bible, Christians only knew two sorts of people: Christians and anti-Christians. A third category could simply not exist because all peoples stemmed from Adam and all had been preached to.

And these legal constructions of just wars were also decisive for the question of slavery. Slavery as such was a widespread practice in medieval Europe and considered a necessary institution for any civilized state. Without a class of dependent workers the ancient city states could neither have been erected nor maintained. And the higher classes would not have been able to live the contemplative life Aristotle and Plato had described as necessary for a civilization. The institution of slavery, then, came from the Greeks to the Romans and, eventually, to Christianity (Pagden, 1982: 41). For centuries the Spaniards had enslaved Muslims on a regular basis and when this source dried out they imported slaves from the Balkans and the Black Sea. However, the legal justification for this kind of slavery was neither that these people were meant to be slaves by their very nature, nor – at least not directly – that they adhered to a different religion. Theoretically, all human beings were free but those like infidels (Muslims) or schismatics (Greeks and Russians) who were taken prisoners in a *just* war could be enslaved rather than killed (Pagden, 1982: 32). This, of course, did not mean that the buyer always had to ascertain that the slave he bought was indeed taken prisoner in a just war. It was enough, as Vitoria pointed out in a letter to Fray Bernardino de Vique with respect to black slaves from Africa, that the person was a slave either 'in fact or in law':

> I see no reason why the gentlemen who purchased them [the African slaves] here in Spain should have any scruples.... for the Portuguese are not obliged to discover the justice of wars between barbarians. It suffices that a man is a slave in fact or in law, and I shall buy him without qualm.... If treated humanely, it would be better for them to be slaves among Christians than free in their own lands; in addition, it is the greatest good fortune to become Christians.
>
> (Vitoria, 1991: 334f)

Similarly, Las Casas originally did not find any principled fault in suggesting to the Crown to use African slaves rather than Amerindians. He had experienced the extraordinary death rates among the Amerindians who were forced to work for the Spaniards and believed that Africans would be stronger and survive the hard work better than the former. He only changed his mind when he discovered that the Africans suffered and died just as the Amerindians had (Las Casas, 1971a: 257). At this point, Las Casas suggested that the increasing demand for African slaves in America which was catered to by the Portuguese slave traders actually led to an increase of wars in Africa; if that was the case, the African wars could not any longer be considered just wars and the Spaniards and Portuguese were morally responsible for the injury done to Africans (Las Casas, 1971b: 102). In light of these arguments it seems clear that in reality the slaves on the European markets were not necessarily prisoners taken in just wars; nevertheless, legally they were.

The first reaction to the American phenomenon, not surprisingly, was the attempt to grasp it with and fit it into the pre-existing worldview and legal categories. Cristóbal Colón was, in this as in other respects, perfectly in line with the medieval worldview and its practices. Colón sailed west not in order to discover something 'new', but in order to find a new route to something 'old', something which was taken for granted, which was part and parcel of the medieval world view and the medieval maps: Asia and its riches and pagans. Colón, deeply influenced by Franciscan teaching which presented him with the challenge to put his search for wealth into the service of religion, became Christopher Columbus – Christopher, the saint who carried Christ over the water. But Franciscan teaching did not just provide him with the general opportunity to put his search for wealth in the service of religion. It provided him with a much more specific vision, for the Franciscans relied strongly on the Apocalypse, the Book of Revelations, which speculated on the signs which might herald the end of the world, of a miserable human existence, of the punishment for human sins. Among these signs for the coming of the end of the world was a last emperor who defended Christianity against the infidel hordes, recaptured Jerusalem and eventually converted the whole human race to Christianity (Flint, 1992: 192). The Spanish Crown, in desperate need of money, in fear of further Muslim attacks, but also extremely optimistic about its seminal role in defeating the infidels and liberating the Iberian peninsula from them, would clearly be quite taken by this line of thought. Colón saw himself as the instrument for the realization of this divine providence: the riches he would find in Asia would allow the Spanish Crown to fit out the last crusade to recapture Jerusalem and convert the whole of the human race to Christianity (Todorov, 1999: 8–13; Flint, 1992: 201).

Since Colón intended to reach the lands of the Great Khan (China), on arrival in the Caribbean he, not surprisingly, believed that that was exactly where he was. Although he was not certain whether he was confronted with islands or mainland, and which particular island might be Cipangu (Japan), which stretch of land might be the mainland of Cathay, whether Hispaniola (Haiti) was in fact the land of the biblical queen of Saba, and how many leagues exactly he was away from the lands of the Great Khan, he maintained that he was just off the coast of the Asian continent (Flint, 1992: 115, 125, 128, 130; Parry, 1981: 150). Moreover, he was convinced that he had seen the legendary Sirens off the coast of Hispaniola, that Martinique was the island of the Amazons, and he believed tales of dog-headed people, of people with only one eye as well as cannibals and other monstrous races (Flint, 1992: 138–44). Only on the third voyage did Colón start to entertain doubts. And the trigger for these doubts was the discovery of the mouth of the Orinoco. Finding no evidence for the existence of such a great river in the scriptures, Colón considered two possibilities: either he was close to a huge landmass of which Europeans hitherto had had no knowledge, or he had discovered the terrestrial paradise.

All this provides great evidence of the earthly Paradise, because the situation agrees with the beliefs of those holy and wise theologians and all the signs strongly accord with this idea. For I have never read or heard of such a quantity of fresh water flowing so close to the salt and flowing into it, and the very temperate climate provides a further confirmation. If this river does not flow out of the earthly Paradise, the marvel is still greater. For I do not believe that there is as great and deep a river anywhere in the world...I would say that if this river does not spring from Paradise it comes from a vast land lying to the south, of which we have hitherto had no reports. But I am firmly convinced that the earthly Paradise truly lies here, and I rely on the authorities and arguments I have cited.

(Cf. Flint, 1992: 154)

There is no question, here, that to have found a 'vast land' would have been much more of a 'marvel' than it was to find the terrestrial paradise. He solved the puzzle by engaging in the accepted mode of knowledge production, namely he considered carefully the beliefs of the 'holy and wise theologians' and on the basis of their writings he decided that this new phenomenon was much more likely to be the terrestrial paradise, regularly depicted on medieval maps, than an unknown continent (Leed, 1995: 13). And in exactly the same way, the Spanish theologians, lawyers, historians, friars and *conquistadores* first attempted to fit the 'new' world into the pre-existing beliefs of the 'old'. Just as Colón had had no difficulty in believing that he had found monsters, cannibals, Amazons and the like, some people argued that that was indeed what the Amerindians really were. Some of the friars, like José de Acosta, on the other hand, referred to Amerindian legends about a great flood, and argued that on the basis of this evidence the Amerindians did remember *the* Great Flood and, thus, must be descendants of Noah's son Japhet (Mason, 1990: 130ff; Las Casas, 1971a: 68). Another theory held that since according to the Bible all peoples had been preached the Christian faith, the Amerindians must have been exposed to the Christian mission of the apostle Thomas (Sánchez, 1994: 216f). Oviedo, the official Spanish historian, argued that the Amerindians were indeed remnants of the Spanish Visigothic monarchy and had, in addition, been exposed to the Christian mission centuries previously (Hanke, 1974: 40f). The discovery of the great architectural monuments of the Mayas in Yucatan gave rise to the theory that the Romans or Carthaginians must have made their way to America centuries ago, because it seemed impossible that the Amerindians were capable of such impressive architecture (Hanke, 1974: 125).

All these theories were not only attempts to make sense of the American phenomenon within the cultural framework of the Spaniards at the time, they also had political and legal relevance. Because if the Amerindians were sons of Japhet, had been preached the Christian faith by the apostle Thomas or remembered the Flood, then they would fall into the same category as either heretics or pagans in Europe, Asia and Africa. That is, they could be considered 'enemies' of the Christian faith who stubbornly resisted the spread of Christianity and against whom, therefore, wars could be justified. If they were remnants of the Spanish Visigothic monarchy or if the Roman Empire had extended to America, then their lands could be considered inalienable Christian territory and the Spaniards would be perfectly justified in reconquering it and establishing their rule there.

However, in the long run these theories were not very convincing. Neither Vitoria, nor Las Casas or Sepúlveda put them forward in the discussion on the legitimacy of wars against the Amerindians, their enslavement or Spanish rule in America. But with the acknowledgement that the Amerindians were, indeed, not peoples ever mentioned in the authoritative writings of Christianity, and as a result not peoples to whom the Christian faith had been preached before, the legal constructions at the disposal of the Spaniards for just wars, crusades, slavery and rule became irrelevant. The justification of the crusades against the Muslims could not be applied to the Amerindians because the Amerindians had never illegally conquered Christian territory. Similarly, the justification of the missionary expeditions into the Baltic or any other pagan region rested on the assumption that these peoples had previous knowledge of Christianity. For both Las Casas and Vitoria there was no question, therefore, that the Amerindians did not fulfil the conditions spelled out in just war theories of having inflicted 'harm' on the Spaniards (Las Casas, 1971a: 8; Vitoria, 1991: 250f). If it was accepted, however, that the Amerindians had never even heard of the Christian religion before, their conversion to Christianity could not necessarily be conducted with the means of war. If it was, thus, extremely questionable whether the Spaniards could lead a just war against the Amerindians, it was consequently also doubtful whether they could enslave them. For, after all, slavery was theoretically only possible for prisoners taken in a just war. And the establishment of Spanish rule in America brought the long-debated basis of political rule as such, and its relationship to spiritual rule, back onto the agenda. Only now, this problem had to be solved on a much more fundamental level, that is without recourse to the Christian religion as an assumed common basis for humanity, either because the political communities in question were Christian, or because they had previous knowledge of Christianity. The Spaniards did simply not have categories which could be applied to the Amerindians (Pagden, 1982: 37).

Unlike the Portuguese who for reasons of climate and the resistance of the native population did not attempt to colonize Africa, the Spaniards found themselves compelled to work out the proper legal relationship between themselves and the Amerindians who, after all, in the course of the colonization of America became subjects of the Spanish Crown and, hence, like other subjects entitled to protection by the Crown (Parry, 1981: 323). And unlike 'barbarians' in the Baltic area, for instance, whose subordination was based on the assumption that they were 'enemies' of Christianity, this assumption did not seem to apply to the Amerindians. And finally, it could not very well be argued that the Amerindians had illegally conquered Christian territory, like the Muslims. Hence, the Spaniards had to work out new categories which might fit the case of the Amerindians. But, as we have seen before, the legal categories of the Europeans were traditionally based on a culturally specific understanding of the nature of human beings, their history and destiny. The discovery of the Amerindians thus challenged these fundamental beliefs. In the course of the attempt to work out new categories which might fit the Amerindian case, the Spaniards found themselves forced to develop or adjust their traditional understanding of human nature, history and destiny in general. And they had to determine the nature of the Amerindians in particular. Only then, after having answered this ontological question, as we shall see in the next chapter, could a solution to the concrete legal and political questions of the justification for war, slavery and Spanish rule in America be found.

3
Reinventing the State of Nature

It was for the observer, as two Spanish travellers put it,

> no easy task to exhibit a true picture of the customs and inclinations of the Indians...for should he form his judgement from their first actions, he must necessarily conclude them to be a people of the greatest penetration and vivacity. But when he reflects on their rudeness, the absurdity of their opinions, and their beastly manner of living, his ideas must take a different turn, and represent them in a degree little above brutes.
>
> (Cf. Hanke, 1974: 139)

This, the exhibition of 'a true picture of the customs and inclinations of the Indians', was exactly the task which those participants in the Spanish debate faced who did not argue that the Amerindians were descendants of Noah or subjects of the former Roman Empire. They had to formulate legal categories for their interaction with the Amerindians based *not* on traditional Christian assumptions. The Spaniards had to solve three problems: firstly, their religious beliefs and worldview were profoundly challenged by the discovery of America and, thus, had to be either defended or adjusted. But since cultures frequently accommodate contradictory concepts this general need would not necessarily have led to the discussion which followed if it had not been for the more concrete issues that needed to be solved. The more concrete second problem, then, arose out of the specific interests the Spaniards pursued in America. And those interests, the accumulation of wealth and the conversion of pagans, created the direct pressure to come up with new legal categories which could be applied to the American case. Finally, this very concrete objective created in turn the need to develop a secular conception of 'international relations'. Indeed, since the Amerindians and the Spaniards neither shared human nor divine law, there was only one kind of law left which might provide a basis for this new conception of 'international relations': natural law.

> The truth of the Gospels and the Decalogue, the primacy of the normative behaviour of the Christians and the rightness of the political and social institutions of Europe had all to be defended, without recourse to arguments from revelation, as the inescapable conclusions of the rational mind drawing upon certain self-evident first principles. In practice this meant that their principal task, as they saw it, was to provide an exegesis of the law of nature – the *ius naturae*.
>
> (Pagden, 1982: 61)

Faced with this task, the Spaniards succeeded in working out at least the starting point for a secular understanding of 'international relations'. What I want to demonstrate in this chapter, however, is the centrality of culture to this new secular understanding of 'international relations'. As we saw in the last chapter, traditionally the religious, Christian, belief had provided a culturally specific understanding of the nature, history and destiny of humankind on which operative legal and political principles were based. The secularization of 'international relations', its regrounding in natural rather than divine law, however, did not and, I will argue, could not, dispose of the need to provide such a specific understanding of human nature, history and destiny. This, in the broadest sense, cultural underpinning for any legal, political or social theory is indispensable; it is theoretically and practically impossible to develop legal, political and social theories and rules without a normative framework in which they make sense and which they, indeed, serve. Consequently, in the course of this debate the Spaniards were compelled to replace the religious worldview underpinning their traditional understanding of international relations with a new cultural worldview to underpin the emerging secular, natural law based conception of international relations.

The first problem which presented itself to the Spaniards was to determine the 'nature' of the Amerindians since they obviously were neither Christians nor enemies of Christianity and, hence, not part of humankind in its traditional religious conception. And if we recall that the medieval worldview easily and as a matter of course accommodated monsters, Amazons, giants, mythical creatures and the like, it might appear less offensive and counterintuitive for our modern minds that the question whether the Amerindians were human beings at all was seriously raised and had to be seriously discussed (Las Casas, 1971a: 8, 68; Vitoria, 1991: 250ff). But what were the possibilities? If one could not use any arguments based on revelation, where could one go to find alternatives? In this respect, the Spaniards were in a fortunate position, for their canon of authoritative scriptures included ancient writers who had not been Christians and did not argue, therefore, by recourse to revelation.

Thus, in a first attempt to establish the nature of the Amerindians the Spaniards tried to apply Aristotle's concept of natural slavery, according to which people without reason could not have *dominium* – that is power/property *de facto* or *de jure* – over their own bodies, their fellow beings, or the material world (Vitoria, 1991: 239). For among human beings there are some

> who by nature are masters and others who by nature are slaves. Those who surpass the rest in prudence and intelligence, although not in physical strength, are by nature the masters. On the other hand, those who are dim-witted and mentally lazy, although they may be physically strong enough to fulfill all the necessary tasks, are by nature slaves.
>
> (Sepúlveda, 1994: 321)

Sepúlveda, thus, returned to the ancient Greek distinction between barbarism and civilization and proposed that Aristotle's definition of natural slaves might fit the Amerindians (Hanke, 1974: 85; Grisel, 1976: 318). Since *dominium rerum*, the right to property, which depended on sufficient reason, did not just describe the capability of human beings to own and use things but their absolute right to give them away, to sell them, to neglect them, the Amerindians, if they could be shown to lack sufficient reason, would not have had the right to own their land, their movable property or even their own bodies (Pagden, 1990: 17, 20). This would have been an ingenious solution to the Spanish problem, for it would have provided the Spaniards with a secular, 'natural', non-Christian justification for the enslavement of the Amerindians and the establishment of Spanish rule in America. Not only that, but it would even have been a moral duty for the Spaniards because it would clearly have been in the interests of the Amerindians to be subjected to Spanish rule since, as the *conquistador* Lucas Vazquez de Ayllon put it, 'it was far better they should become slave men [*hombres siervos*] than to remain free beasts [*bestias libras*]' (cf. Hanke, 1974: 10). After all, for the 'barbarians' it 'ought to be even more advantageous than for the Spaniards, since virtue, humanity, and the true religion are more valuable than gold or silver' (Sepúlveda, 1994: 323).

It was not just Sepúlveda, though very much applauded by the *conquistadores* whose interests would have been served very well indeed if this position had been adopted, who seriously considered Aristotle's concept of natural slavery. Las Casas and Vitoria equally discussed the applicability of this concept (Vitoria, 1991: 240ff; Las Casas, 1971b: 144f). Vitoria distinguished between potentially four different grounds on which it might be argued that the Amerindians were natural slaves: namely 'that they were either sinners [*peccatores*], unbelievers [*infideles*], madmen [*amentes*], or insensate [*insensati*]' (Vitoria, 1991: 240). Probing into all four possibilities, Vitoria maintained that in so far as *dominium*, the right to property *de jure* and *de facto*, was based on human law, a sinner who insulted God did not lose his property rights; even in Christian states, sinners did not lose their property rights (1991: 242f). Furthermore, since all forms of *dominium* stem from either human or natural law, they could not be annulled because of a lack of the true faith either and, indeed, the Spaniards did not deny property rights to Jews or Muslims (1991: 244ff). Vitoria, hence, rejected arguments based on religion and was left with the need to establish whether the Amerindians were by nature lacking in reason like either madmen or children.

Las Casas also provided four potential definitions for Aristotle's concept of barbarism. A barbarian could, firstly, be someone who behaved in a brutal and uncontrolled way. Secondly, one could call a people barbarian if it either did not know how to write or did not speak properly (this, he claims, was the meaning of the term for the Greeks for whom those who did not speak Greek were barbarians). Thirdly, one could call barbarians 'those who ... appear cruel and ferocious, remote from other men and not ruling themselves by reason.... They neither have nor care for law, right, nation, friendship, or the company of other men, because of which they lack towns, councils, and cities, since they do not live socially' (Las Casas, 1971b: 144f). This group is, according to Las Casas, the group which Aristotle defined as natural slaves. In its fourth meaning, all those peoples can be called barbarous who did not have the true Christian religion. Las Casas rejected the first category, that of madmen, because one could not conceive of a whole people being mad, and he rejected the second category arguing that although the Amerindians did not speak Spanish properly, neither did the Spaniards speak the Amerindian languages properly. This was, therefore, a relative category. They were clearly barbarians in the sense that they lacked literacy, though, and in the sense that they were unbelievers. But since, unlike the Moors and the Jews, they had no knowledge of the true religion and, so far, had neither fought nor resisted it, they could not be punished for it. The fact that they were barbarians in these two senses meant that they needed to be taught the Christian faith and, possibly, writing. It did not, however, establish that they were not capable of governing themselves, that they were 'natural slaves' who were incapable of living an ordered social life (Las Casas, 1971b: 145f; Hanke, 1974: 76).

Vitoria, Las Casas and Sepúlveda agreed, then, that what needed to be established was whether the Amerindians demonstrated a sufficient amount of reason to govern themselves. Now, for the Spaniards, reason was the ability to understand the laws of nature and to apply this knowledge in the way men dealt with nature and with one another. According to this view, humanity must now conform to a 'natural' rather than a religious order. Yet, this order does not yet exist in reality. It has to be created by human beings and is, thus, like the traditional religious order, a normative obligation. Again, therefore, the basis for the legal and political concepts is a culturally very specific definition of human nature, history and destiny. Specifically, the Spaniards needed to test whether the Amerindians followed their 'natural' obligation to realize the 'natural' hierarchy from inorganic matter through plants and animals to human beings on the highest level, i.e. to control the external as well as their own internal nature – in fact, to turn nature into culture (Bitterli, 1982: 216). What the Spaniards needed to demonstrate, then, was whether the Amerindians lived socially and, if so, whether their social arrangements, their societal institutions, reflected an understanding and an attempt to implement, to realize, this 'natural' order. And, indeed, they applied this test to a whole range of social and political institutions from food to war, from sex to literacy, from production to government.

One of the most basic necessities that drive human beings to interact with nature, of course, is food. For the Spaniards, the choice and preparation of food was indicative of the level of reason. For any reasonable person would understand the 'natural hierarchy' and, thus, know that, generally speaking, the lower forms of life were there for the use of the ones on the next higher stage – plants were food for animals and animals were food for human beings. To respect this hierarchy meant that human beings were to eat, ideally, the meat of animals. In addition, human beings were supposed to eat food cooked not raw, for in nature things only existed *in potentia* and human beings had to actualize that potential, they had to transform nature into culture. There was no question for Vitoria that 'God shows the natural custom for eating meat, that is to say cooked not raw, since any other custom is barbarous and savage' (Vitoria, 1991: 209). Las Casas, too, believed that the only kind of food that could be taken raw was milk, since drinking the mother's milk could not well be deemed against natural law (Pagden, 1982: 89). The preparation of food, its transformation from natural potential to cultural actuality, in addition, occupied a central place in the ritual of transubstantiation in which bread is turned into Christ's body and wine into his blood.

It was, then, for the Spaniards a sign of reason to eat cooked meat. Tomás Ortiz, however, reported to the Council of the Indies that the Amerindians ate 'fleas, spiders, and worms raw, whenever they find them' (cf. Hanke, 1964: 51). If this was true, the Amerindians had placed themselves, in the eyes of the Spanish observers, unwittingly on the same level as those animals who, as a general rule, ate fleas, spiders and worms for

> the quality of the thing being eaten reflects the quality of the eater. Thus it is 'better' to eat a cow than a cabbage for precisely the same reason that . . . it is better to command a woman than a donkey. The better a man is the better and the more complex will be the things over which he has authority, the food he eats, the house he lives in and so on. The Indians who eat frogs and forage for roots are little different from the brute animals with which they have to compete for their sustenance.
>
> (Pagden, 1982: 88).

But the Amerindians were reported to commit an even worse sin: they were supposed to eat 'human flesh' and practise human sacrifice (Sepúlveda, 1994: 322). These 'facts' were accepted by all discussants. Cannibalism, argued Vitoria, violated not only the dietary laws and the laws of a well ordered society because it presupposed the killing of members of one's own species, as did human sacrifice, but also the right of every human being to a decent burial (Vitoria, 1991: 210). However, in so far as these rights and laws were derived from God, they could not be applied to the Amerindian case. If Vitoria wanted to reject the 'cannibalism' of the Amerindians he had to demonstrate that it constituted a violation of natural law. And this he did by maintaining that cannibalism violated the *ius gentium*, international or natural law

(Vitoria, 1991: 207). Cannibalism was against natural law, understood as the customary law based on the consensus of all civilized peoples (1991: 209). Although the Bible as well as numerous authors of antiquity report examples of peoples practising cannibalism, Vitoria maintained that all these authors denounced the practice in their writings and called it an inhuman act of barbarism. 'The deduction from the premiss is proved because a thing is said to be against natural law when it is universally held by all to be unnatural' (1991: 209). In other words, only peoples who do not practise cannibalism are civilized and because all civilized peoples agree that cannibalism is barbarous, to put it polemically, it is not just against divine law but also against natural law (1991: 210).

For Sepúlveda, too, there was no question that one could not expect much reason 'from men who were involved in every kind of intemperance and wicked lust and who used to eat human flesh' (cf. Hanke, 1974: 85). Las Casas, however, argued that these practices just proved the potential reason of the Amerindians for they had obviously understood that the greatest sacrifice one could give to God was human life. Not only did the Bible and other ancient texts mention human sacrifice quite frequently, but Christians, after all, celebrated the human sacrifice of Jesus every Sunday in mass where they incidentally also – metaphorically – ate his flesh and drank his blood (Las Casas, 1971b: 186ff; Pagden, 1982: 88; Hanke, 1974: 93f).

In the realm of production, too, the Spaniards defined the mastery of nature, the realization of its potential through human labour as a clear sign of reason. Technology, therefore, and the production of tools for agriculture and handicrafts were an important standard of measurement for the reason of the Amerindians. The fact that almost all Amerindian societies practised some kind of agriculture and were advanced in handicrafts was enough evidence for Las Casas that they had reason (Las Casas, 1971b: 115). Sepúlveda, on the other hand, argued that 'even though some of them show a talent for certain handicrafts, this is not an argument in favor of a more human skill, since we see that some small animals, both birds and spiders, make things which no human industry can imitate completely' (cf. Hanke, 1974: 85). For Sepúlveda and others some kind of agriculture or handicrafts was not enough to prove that the Amerindians satisfactorily exploited the natural potential of the soil, that they indeed turned nature into culture (Pagden, 1982: 91). In particular, iron for the production of tools and weapons was considered absolutely essential and, of course, lacking in America.

The perceived lack of a work ethic among the Amerindians only supported their low score in the realm of production. They were generally considered to be lazy. This conviction was so deeply rooted with the Spaniards that Oviedo could actually describe the horrendous labour conditions imposed on the Amerindians and then conclude that they frequently committed suicide because of their 'lazyness' and as a 'pastime'.

> The mines being rich and man's greed insatiable, some [Spaniards] worked their Indians excessively, others failed to feed them properly. Indians are born lazy, idle, melancholy and cowardly, vile and ill-natured, liars, with a short memory and no perseverance. As a pastime many took poison in order to avoid work, others hanged themselves and others died in the epidemic of small pox that spread over the whole island. Thus, in a short time, they were all gone.
>
> (Cf. Las Casas, 1971b: 274)

Not only did the Amerindians not show much enthusiasm for work in the eyes of the Spaniards but they demonstrated a maddening lack of understanding for the 'objective' value of certain material objects as well as of the social value to be derived from wealth. 'They prize bird feathers of various colours, beads made of fish bones, and green and white stones with which they adorn their ears and lips, but they put no value on gold and other precious things' (Las Casas, 1971a: 64). Gold, in particular, did not just have material value for the Spaniards which could be translated into a higher social status, but it also had a spiritual quality. Europeans believed in the magic qualities of gold which could overcome the separation between the spiritual and the material world. Hence, countless alchemists in Europe attempted to find a way of producing gold and, thus, to lift the veil of the secret of life (Sheehan, 1980: 13ff; Sanchez, 1994: 189ff). And unlike the Spaniards who could raise their social status with the help of wealth – that is, by commanding women rather than donkeys, or men rather than women, the more the better – many Amerindian societies did not practise this kind of social stratification.

In addition, notions of property differed widely from the Spanish ones so that the same phenomenon which led Oviedo to call them pathological thieves was interpreted by Las Casas in quite the opposite way, namely that 'they are extremely generous with their possessions and by the same token covet the possessions of their friends and expect the same degree of liberality' (Las Casas, 1971a: 64). Furthermore, the way in which the Amerindians conducted 'trade' confused the Spaniards from the moment they set foot onto American soil. For, on the one hand, 'trade' in the form of gift-giving was interpreted by the Spaniards as the absence of property and as extreme generosity. On the other hand, the Spaniards did not grasp that gift-giving involved the establishment of a long-term relationship in which, at some later point, a gift was expected in return. Hence, the seeming generosity of the Amerindians on the one hand, and their tough and prudent negotiations on the other seemed to contradict each other (Sheehan, 1980: 135ff).

Just as the Spaniards assumed the hierarchy between animals and human beings as natural, so they also assumed the authority of men over women, fathers over children, the elders over the young ones, as central to natural law (Todorov, 1999: 153; Pagden, 1982: 44). Sepúlveda held that the Amerindians were 'as inferior to the Spaniards as infants to adults and women to men' (Sepúlveda, 1994: 322). The institution of the family and the relations between the sexes had to be organized accordingly. The institution of the family was absolutely central, for it was considered the cell, the basic unit, of a properly ordered society. Matrilocal and matrilinear Amerindian societies in which the women played a considerable and independent role and had responsibility for the education of the children clearly did not recognize this natural hierarchy (Hanke, 1964: 51; Pagden, 1982: 52f).

This problem was confounded, on the one hand, by the widespread practice of nakedness or near nakedness in Amerindian societies, as well as by the quite frequent custom of communal houses. Communal houses did not, in the eyes of the Spaniards, allow for the proper spatial distance between the sexes, between generations, and between different families. The Spaniards, like Tomás Ortiz, concluded frequently from this set up that the Amerindians 'are more given to sodomy than any other nation', that they had 'no respect for virginity... Husbands observe no fidelity towards their wives, nor the wives towards their husbands' (cf. Hanke, 1964: 51). The Amerindians were systematically accused of sodomy, incest, homosexuality and other 'perversions', all of which demonstrated that they did not observe the natural law according to which neither animals and human beings nor members of the same sex or members of the same family could become sexual partners (Pagden, 1982: 86). And yet, the same facts were again interpreted by Las Casas in a very different way when he maintained that

> marriage laws are nonexistent; men and women alike choose their mates and leave them as they please, without offense, jealousy or anger. They multiply in great abundance; pregnant women work to the last minute and give birth almost painlessly; up the next day they bathe in the river and are as clean and healthy as before giving birth.

> If they tire of their men, they give themselves abortions with herbs that force stillbirths, covering their shameful parts with leaves or cotton cloths; although on the whole, Indian men and women look upon total nakedness with as much casualness as we look upon a man's head or at his hands. In addition, they bathe frequently and keep very clean.
>
> (Las Casas, 1971a: 64)

There was no question for Las Casas that marriage laws and fidelity were a necessary feature of a civilized society, just as abortions and nakedness were out of the question. Unlike Sepúlveda, however, he insisted that innocence, not decadence, were at the root of such behaviour, for 'they treat women so decently no one in the world would mind seeing them together' (Las Casas, 1971a: 64).

If social relations on the basic level of the family seemed to contradict what the Spaniards took to be the 'natural' order of things, it comes as no surprise that Amerindian political organization also posed a challenge to this order. There were, on the one hand, those societies which seemed to lack any kind of hierarchy. For, as Thevet summarized later:

> There are no men so beastly, wild and cruel as these men are, who have never savored another obedience than that which they impose upon one another, without any royalty or principality existing among them; when going to war, however, they choose one amongst themselves, to whom the others pay their respect and whom they obey.
>
> (Cf. Mason, 1994: 142f)

Vasco de Quiroga, too, argued that those egaliatarian communities or village republics could not count as properly organized societies because they lacked the institution of private property and, hence, the community counted for more than the individuals. Proper laws as the basis of a properly organized political community were derived from private property and the latter institution was restricted to people 'who at least know and observe the natural law, do not worship many gods, and have a king and an ordered politic life' (cf. Pagden, 1990: 26). Those Amerindian communities which were taken to be ruled by warlords he considered as oligarchies who only served the private interests of the ruler. The Aztec Empire, on the other hand, was seen as a tyranny because its ruler was not hailed by a free people as a king, but considered a god by an oppressed population. Similarly, the election of rulers, a quite common feature in Amerindian societies, was seen as neither legitimate nor reasonable but rather tyrannical (Pagden, 1990: 26). So, too, Sepúlveda maintained that

> they have established their commonwealth in such a manner that no one individually owns anything, neither a house nor a field that one may dispose of or leave to his heirs in his will, because everything is controlled by their lords who are incorrectly called kings. They live more at the mercy of their king's will than of their own. They are the slaves of his will and caprice, and they are not the masters of their fate. The fact that this condition is not the result of coercion but is voluntary and spontaneous is a certain sign of the servile and base spirit of these barbarians.
>
> (Sepúlveda, 1994: 323)

The absence of writing confounded the problem for, as we have seen, in Spanish culture 'nothing could be made intelligible in terms of an alternative non-scriptural authority' (Pagden, 1993: 52). Writing was considered a precondition for a civilized society in which the common interests were derived from universally valid and abstract principles (Pagden, 1993: 135f.). What was decisive for Sepúlveda, therefore, was the absence of *written* laws and of a *written* history, because oral or pictorial accounts of history and law appealed to emotions rather than reason. Hence, they were not law or history in the proper sense but only 'barbarous institutions and customs' (Sepúlveda, 1994: 322). Las Casas, seconded by Vitoria (Vitoria, 1991: 250), on the other hand, argued that

> they have important kingdoms, large numbers of people who live settled lives in a society, great cities, kings, judges and laws, persons who engage in commerce, buying, selling, lending, and the other contracts of the law of nations... Rather, long before they had heard the word Spaniard, they had properly organized states, wisely ordered by excellent laws, religion, and customs.
>
> (Cf. Hanke, 1974: 75f)

Finally, the truly unreasonable character of the Amerindians clearly comes to light, according to Sepúlveda, in the relations between political communities in America.

> And you must realize that prior to the arrival of the Christians, they did not live in that peaceful kingdom of Saturn that the poets

imagine, but on the contrary they made war against one another continually and fiercely, with such fury that victory was of no meaning if they did not satiate their monstrous hunger with the flesh of their enemies... These Indians are so cowardly and timid that they could scarcely resist the mere presence of our soldiers. Many times thousands upon thousands of them scattered, fleeing like women before a very few Spaniards, who amounted to fewer than a hundred.

(Sepúlveda, 1994: 322f)

The Amerindians were, on the one hand, 'continually and fiercely' making war, while on the other, they were like women, cowards who ran away from the Spaniards. In the eyes of Sepúlveda, essentially two aspects of their presumed behaviour in war clearly demonstrated their lack of reason. Firstly, they lost their wars against the Spaniards. The Spanish success in the Mexican conquest, for instance, is taken by Sepúlveda as a clear indication of the superiority of the Spaniards, for, he asked, 'can there be a greater or stronger testimony how some men surpass others in talent, industry, strength of mind, and valor? Or that such peoples are slaves by nature?' (cf. Hanke, 1974: 85). The Amerindians clearly had not been able to make such successful use of the mechanical laws of nature – in designing guns, for instance – as to withstand the Spaniards (Pagden, 1990: 25f.). Secondly, the Amerindians supposedly went to war for no other reason than their totally unrestrained rage and lust for human flesh accompanied by an equally unrestrained fear and cowardice which made them like women. In contrast, Europeans were supposedly living 'in harmony and concord with each other – or at least in situations of carefully regulated violence – and ruled their lives according to an established code of law' (Pagden, 1982: 20). Quite in line with this kind of reading of the nature of Christian as well as Amerindian behaviour in respect to other political communities, Cortés called his conquests 'pacification' and justified them as such in his letters to the Crown (1986: 63). But, again, Las Casas provided a different interpretation of the same facts. For although he also insisted on the peacefulness and harmony which prevailed among the Amerindians (Las Casas, 1971a: 155), he did not deny the internal divisions in the case of Mexico. But he insisted that

Cortés was pleased to find enmity among the Indians, for it served his purpose well. These are thoughts and desires entertained by tyrants who use such enmity better to subjugate both parties, as he did.

Tyrants act with a bad conscience; they lack reason, right and justice, as the Philosopher says in Book V, Chapter II of the *Politics*. They take advantage of discords when these exist or otherwise they create them to divide people and subject them more easily, because they know it is more difficult, sometimes impossible, to subject a people united in conformity... and better to deceive the world he [Cortés] said he was helping the one against the other, as if he had heard both parties and as a competent judge would determine which was in the wrong. ... he could not judge either *de iure* or *de facto*.

(Las Casas, 1971a: 241)

What this debate demonstrates is that every single aspect of societal life, for the Spaniards, was governed by a particular meaning of human history and destiny, in other words by a particular culture which was supposedly rooted in nature and, thus, universally valid. The concrete central feature of this culture was the assumption that to become human meant to realize and implement a particular order in nature and society. Human beings, however, had to use their reason in order to come to 'know' this order as their goal, its implementation as their moral obligation in life, since in nature it only existed as a potential.

It ought to be noted at this point that the Spaniards did not, in fact, believe that all the ideals against which they measured the Amerindian societal institutions were actually realized in Spain itself. Far from it. The majority of Spaniards at the time did, of course, not have a diet of 'cooked meat', did not necessarily abstain from adultery or homosexuality, did not work in the mines or on the fields – Spain was dry and barren and the main sources of income were connected with sheep – and certainly Spain did not live in peace and harmony with its neighbours but had been involved in constant military expeditions. Yet, however much the kinds of judgements the Spaniards made about the Amerindians might therefore seem entirely unfair to us, there is nonetheless a very serious content to them. The decisive difference was not whether people actually lived up to their ideals but whether there was any sign of these ideals being recognized. The complaints about the laziness of the Amerindians, for instance, did not imply that the *conquistadores* were workaholics. On the contrary, according to Las Casas they were too lazy even to walk and let their Amerindian workers carry them (Las Casas, 1971a: 79). But this very fact demonstrated that Spanish society was organized along hierarchical lines. It entailed a division of labour in which certain people were meant to work in the field, for instance, and others were meant to go to war, certain people commanded men, others sheep, and yet other groups, like women, slaves and children, did not command anything at all but obeyed. The *conquistadores* in general came either from the (lower) aristocracy who were not born to work in the first instance, or had only come to America in order to move up into this very class. In this light, the *conquistadores* did in fact undertake the kind of work which they considered appropriate either for their position in society or for their aspirations, that is they continuously led wars against the Amerindians, engaged ceaselessly in slave-hunting expeditions and explored the land – all this, clearly, under the most difficult and trying circumstances and with a great deal of courage (1971a: 154–7). Furthermore, the contemplative life of the upper classes was considered the only truly civilized life in the ancient Greek writings just as much as in Spain in the fifteenth and sixteenth centuries. And this is exactly Sepúlveda's defence against the argument, put forward by Las Casas, for instance, that the Spaniards themselves did, in actual fact, not show much 'civilization' in comparison with the Amerindians. Sepúlveda refers

> in general terms only to those Spaniards who have received a liberal education. If some of them are wicked and unjust, that is no reason to denigrate the glory of their race, which should be judged by the actions of its cultivated and noble men and by its customs and public institutions, rather than by the actions of depraved persons who are similar to slaves.
>
> (Sepúlveda, 1994: 322)

Hence, it is the institutional difference and, in particular, the absence of this civilized upper class in the social hierarchy which distinguishes Amerindian from Spanish society.

No matter what position the respective discussants reached in the end, to start with there was a clear consensus on the validity of the test, the standards of measurement, and, as became apparent in the course of the discussion, even on the 'facts'. Las Casas argued:

> These peoples have excellent, subtle and very capable minds ... They are likewise prudent, and endowed by nature with the three kinds of prudence named by the Philosopher [Aristotle]: monastic, economic, and political prudence includes the six parts which, according to Aristotle, make any republic self-sufficient and prosperous: farmers;

craftsmen; warriors; men of wealth; priests...; and sixth, judges or ministers of justice or men who govern well.

(Las Casas, 1971b: 115)

Vitoria agreed:

> They have some order [*ordo*] in their affairs: they have properly organized cities, proper marriages, magistrates and overlords [*domini*], laws, industries, and commerce, all of which require the use of reason. They likewise have a form [*species*] of religion, and they correctly apprehend things which are evident to other men, which indicates the use of reason.

(Vitoria, 1991: 250)

And even Sepúlveda never once doubted that the Amerindians had developed 'political and social institutions... rationally planned cities and non-hereditary kings who are elected by popular suffrage, and they carry on commerce among themselves in the manner of civilized people' (Sepúlveda, 1994: 323). But while Vitoria drew from these facts the conclusion that 'the barbarians undoubtedly possessed as true dominion, both public and private, as any Christians. That is to say, they could not be robbed of their property, either as private citizens or as princes, on the grounds that they were not true masters [*ueri domini*]' (Vitoria, 1991: 250f), Sepúlveda concluded:

> On the contrary, in those same institutions there is proof of the coarseness, barbarism, and innate servility of these men. Natural necessity encourages the building of houses, some rational manner of life, and some sort of commerce. Such an agreement merely proves that they are neither bears nor monkeys and that they are not totally irrational.

(Sepúlveda, 1994: 323)

But the absence of private property and the voluntary subjection to their ruler proved that they were not rational enough to govern themselves. Notwithstanding the existence of some manner of societal institutions, Sepúlveda argued that

> it will always be just and in conformity with natural law that such people submit to the rule of more cultured and humane princes and nations. Thanks to the virtues and practical wisdom of their laws, the

latter can destroy barbarism and educate these (inferior) people to a more humane and virtuous life. And if the latter reject such rule, it can be imposed upon them by force of arms.

(1994: 321)

Thus, whether the Amerindians were real human beings or natural slaves could not be decided on the basis of the facts. And this is, of course, not too surprising because what the Spaniards essentially tested was the culture of the Amerindians. And culture, in turn, is a matter of meaning, of interpretation, not of facts. That Sepúlveda, Vitoria and Las Casas came up with different interpretations was due to the fact that they had, essentially, chosen different and, indeed, contradictory points of reference from within the Spanish cultural framework. At this point, therefore, the external encounter turned into an internal challenge which did not just divide Spanish society politically but also culturally (Parry, 1990: 159). For it became clear that the external encounter had brought to light contradictory principles within the Spanish cultural framework and, hence, made it necessary to develop a new consensus. As we have seen, Sepúlveda fully identified with Aristotle's view that all the different kinds of 'authority and power' were ultimately derived from 'a single principle', namely that 'the perfect should command and rule over the imperfect, the excellent over its opposite'; and perfection and imperfection, excellency and baseness, were given in nature in general and in the nature of human beings in particular (Sepúlveda, 1994: 321). Vitoria and Las Casas, meanwhile, defended a Christian principle which directly contradicted this assumption, namely the principle of the Christian *oikumene*. The Christians – believing in a common origin of mankind and God's will for the perfection of man and the natural world – had to extend their *oikumene* over the whole world; it was to include all peoples in the end (Pagden, 1982: 16ff). But if this was so, all peoples had to have sufficient reason to grasp the Christian teachings – otherwise the obligation God had given to the Christians would have been contradictory. For this reason, Las Casas argued that 'it was not possible that over such extensive regions so many and innumerable kinds of men should be allowed to be born naturally and all-inclusively monstrous, that is to say, without reason and the ability to govern their domestic affairs' (Las Casas, 1971a: 5). Likewise, Vitoria held that '"God and nature never fail in the things necessary" for the majority of the species, and the chief attribute of man is reason' (Vitoria, 1991: 239).

On the basis of this argument, the Amerindians were eventually considered as human beings endowed with reason. And on the basis of this argument, too, the theory of natural slavery was determined to be heretical. Sepúlveda's manuscript on the Amerindians, *Democrates Alter*, could not be published in Spain and Sepúlveda himself qualified his statement afterwards (Hanke, 1974: 117f; Parry, 1990: 149). Interestingly, though, the consensus, again, was arrived at on the basis of a belief about human destiny, namely that all peoples were to become Christian. It was this belief about the future of humankind which led to a decision about the nature of peoples one was confronted with in the present. With this solution to the question whether the Amerindians were human beings, the Spaniards immediately confronted another set of problems, practical as well as theoretical. Practically, since the Amerindians were now considered human beings and since *dominium*, the right to property and rule, was based on natural rather than divine law, the Amerindian political communities were legal and just and had to be respected. This outcome, of course, presented a huge problem for the Spanish *conquistadores* and friars who by that time had already been in America for fifty years or so, and for the Spanish Crown in whose name they colonized this 'new' continent. Unlike Sepúlveda who had used the Roman term *ius gentium* in its original sense as regulating the relations between individuals, Vitoria applied this term in the course of the debate to the relations between political communities (Parry, 1990: 146). It is in this sense that Vitoria can be considered the founder of modern international law, for in his discussion of the American question he had clearly established rights and obligations of political communities irrespective of religion (Parry, 1981: 307). He had developed the first tentative formulation of a basis for a secular theory of International Relations. And it was Sepúlveda, arguing from a position of individual rather than community rights, just as Liberals do today, whose 'universalist' conception would have made the fate of the Amerindians one of 'natural' slavery.

However, it would be wrong to assume that Vitoria, and even Las Casas, did not see any differences between the Amerindians and the Spaniards. And the fact that they did leads us to the second, the theoretical, problem arising out of the Spanish consensus. For this solution did not at all solve the problem of cultural difference but rather posed it in new terms. For if God had given reason to all peoples how could it be explained that its use led to such different kinds of development as in the European and the Amerindian cases? If reason meant understanding and applying the – by definition universal – laws of nature, it had surely to lead to universal norms, institutions and material achievements. And, as we have seen above, no one in Spain argued that the Amerindian institutions were equal to the Spanish ones. The Spaniards came up with two different answers to this question, both of which – as we shall see later – became foundational for European thought in general and still represent the two dominant understandings of culture in International Relations theory today. Las Casas believed that

> the entire human race is one; all men are alike with respect to their creation and the things of nature, and none is borne already taught. And so we all have the need, from the beginning, to be guided and helped by those who have been borne earlier. Thus, when some very rustic peoples are found in the world, they are like untilled land, which easily produces worthless weeds and thorns, but has within itself so much natural power that when it is plowed and cultivated it gives useful and wholesome fruits.
>
> (Las Casas, 1971b: 201f)

For him, therefore, the Amerindians were men in the state of nature, with the potential of reason but without cultivation, without history – they were born late. And this state of nature was clearly the state of innocence in which all human beings had found themselves before the fall from grace. He described them over and over again as 'a docile and good-natured people, accustomed to the practice of virtue' and claimed that he had not found 'any comparable nation in the world in ancient history, except perhaps the Seres of Asia, who are a peace-loving and gentle people ... , who love justice ... , and who know not how to kill or fornicate, have no prostitutes, adulterers, thieves, or homicides and adore no idols' (Las Casas, 1971a: 66, 155). In this view, the Amerindians lived the social life of paradise without any of the cultural devices, like government and property, which God had introduced for the punishment of sin. The minds of the Amerindians, for Las Casas, were a cultural vacuum which – because of their potential for reason – would readily grasp and apply the teachings of the Spaniards (1971a: 278).

Vitoria, on the other hand, did not see them without history, culture or sin – on the contrary:

> Nor could it be their fault if they were so many thousands of years outside the state of salvation ... Thus if they seem to us insensate and slow-witted, I put it down mainly to their evil and barbarous education. Even amongst ourselves we see many peasants (*rustici*) who are little different from brute animals.
>
> (Vitoria, 1991: 250)

So, Vitoria did not see them as representatives of the innocent original nature of man but denounced their customs as evil, as a product of education, of history, of thousands of years of socialization. Indeed, Vitoria expected that it would take about six hundred years to undo this kind of education (Pagden, 1982: 100). Hence, we have two solutions to the puzzle of cultural difference. Given universal reason, the cultural difference between Spaniards and Amerindians could either be due to the fact that the latter had not yet developed any kind of culture, or due to the fact that they had developed a false culture, one that deviated from natural law.

For all their differences, these positions shared two crucial aspects. Firstly, both construct a hierarchy between the Amerindians and the Spaniards. In the state-of-nature approach this hierarchy rests on the assumption that the Spaniards do have culture while the Amerindians do not, while the false-culture approach implies that the Spaniards have developed the right culture. Secondly, in both cases the assimilation of the Amerindians to Spanish culture became the practical political goal. They only differed with respect to the means necessary, for if the Amerindians did not understand the true nature of the world the exponents of the state-of-nature position held that it was 'not because they lacked reason, but because they lacked culture, not because they lacked the will to learn or a ready mind, but because they had neither tutors nor teachers' (cf. Pagden, 1982: 92). Hence, the Spaniards had to send tutors and teachers. In contrast, those who believed that the minds of the Amerindians were filled with false cultural values and customs held that 'they will never abandon these evils unless they are first punished and subjected by force and wars, and afterwards preached to' (cf. Hanke, 1974: 125, 136).

Given the fact that the Spaniards still needed to justify their interventions into the now, at least theoretically, accepted legal communities of the Amerindians, the cultural differences were an obvious place to start. The debate which followed bears a striking familiarity to contemporary debates on (humanitarian) intervention. Starting from the question whether the cultural difference in itself would be sufficient grounds for intervention, Sepúlveda argued that God and nature gave the Spaniards the right to make war against the Amerindians because of 'their prodigious sacrifice of human victims, the extreme harm that they inflicted on innocent persons, their horrible banquets of human flesh, and the impious cult of their idols', in addition to homosexuality, non-exploitation of natural resources and so on, which were all against natural law (Sepúlveda, 1994: 323; Pagden, 1990: 29; Hanke, 1974: 86).

Vitoria and Las Casas both argued that the Amerindian could not be punished 'by the Church, and much less by Christian rulers, for a crime or a superstition, no matter how abominable...as long as he commits it...within the borders of the territory of his own masters and his own unbelief' (cf. Hanke, 1974: 89; Vitoria, 1991: 274). But, more important than the inviolability of what we would today call the sovereignty of the Amerindians, was their argument that the universal truth and validity of natural law could not be proven (Vitoria, 1991: 275, 217f; Hanke, 1974: 93ff). Nevertheless, both Las Casas and Vitoria agreed in principle with Sepúlveda's argument that there is an obligation to protect the innocent victims of practices contrary to the laws of nature. In practice, however, they held differing views. Las Casas argued that as long as there is consent between the people, their ministers and priests on the question of such practices, they act under an excusable ignorance for which only God can punish them. Furthermore, one could not protect a few victims of human sacrifice by making war against the whole people. This course of action would cost many more lives than the Amerindian customs, and it would not convince the people of their error (Hanke, 1974: 91f, 95). Vitoria, for his part, posited that the obligation to love one's neighbour overrides other considerations even if natural laws cannot be proven. 'It makes no difference that all the barbarians consent to these kinds of rites and sacrifices, or that they refuse to accept the Spaniards as their liberators in that matter' (Vitoria, 1991: 288). Christian rulers can lead a just war against the barbarians on the grounds that such practices 'involve injustice [*iniuria*] to other men' (1991: 225).

The public debate ended with a consensus based on Vitoria's arguments. Since the Amerindians were human beings they had to live according to the laws of nature, one of which being that 'amity [*amiticia*] between men is part of natural law, and that it is against nature to shun the company of harmless men' (1991: 278f). Thus, human beings had the natural right to communication – which was realized in travel, in trade, in settling wherever they wanted and in missionizing. This natural right of the Spaniards was accompanied by the natural obligation of the Amerindians to allow this kind of communication (1991: 279–81). Furthermore, 'since all those peoples are not merely in a state of sin, but presently in a state beyond salvation, it is the business of Christians to correct and direct them. Indeed they are clearly obliged to do so' (1991: 284). Therefore, the Spaniards had not only the right but also the moral obligation to establish communication with the Amerindians. If, on the other hand, the Amerindians denied the Spaniards the right of communication the Spaniards could lead a just war against them (1991:

283f). Despite his own qualms – Vitoria believed that the Spaniards generally did not obey the spirit of these rules but, at best, the letter – he had spelled out the theoretical basis on which the Spanish Crown and the *conquistadores* could justify their wars against the Amerindians (1991: 282, 284, 291, 331ff). After almost fifty years of debate between contending theoretical and political positions, it was the humanitarian obligation of the Spaniards that justified the wars, the *encomienda* system and Spanish rule (Las Casas, 1971a: 127; Vitoria, 1991: 225, 285f; Hanke, 1974: 121). At every step of the way, though, the Spaniards had to make arguments based on cultural beliefs and considerations. And in so far as they developed the basis for a secular understanding of international relations and international law, it clearly contained not just a general statement on the natural rights of political communities but also one on the natural rights and obligations of people to communicate, to trade, to travel, to missionize, to 'help' their neighbours. With the help of this latter rule the Spaniards embarked on a totalizing project of cultural assimilation, as we shall see in the next chapter.

4
The Politics of the State of Nature in the 'New' World

Sepúlveda and his supporters interpreted the biblical parable of the wedding feast as justifying the use of force in bringing the Amerindians into the folds of the Church. This was too much for Las Casas:

> What do joyful tidings have to do with wounds, capitivities, massacres, conflagrations, the destruction of cities, and the common evils of war? They [the Amerindians] will go to hell rather than learning the advantages of the gospel. And what will be told by the fugitives who seek out the provinces of other peoples out of fear of the Spaniards, with their heads split, their hands amputated, their intestines torn open? What will they think about the God of the Christians? They will certainly think that the Spaniards are sons of the devil, not the children of God and the messengers of peace. Would those who interpret that parable in this way, if they were pagans, want the truth to be announced to them after their homes had been destroyed, their children imprisoned, their wives raped, their cities devastated, their maidens deflowered, and their provinces laid waste?
>
> (Cf. Hanke, 1974: 96)

For the theoretical debate analysed in the previous chapter was not just an idle pastime of theologians, scholars and lawyers in Spain. The real stakes in it were unbelievable, ongoing brutalities – the destruction of many cultures and of the indigenous American population in the order of 90 per cent or more. The discourse on the state of nature could not be separated from its practice. In this chapter I will show that the practices of the *conquistadores* as well as the policies of the Crown and those of the missionaries were all directed towards the destruction of the Amerindian cultures, their total assimilation to Spanish culture.

By every reckoning, the conquest of America led to one of the biggest, if not the biggest, demographic catastrophes the world has ever seen (Parry, 1990: 227). In 1500 the world's population was estimated at about 400 million people. Of these, 80 million were indigenous Americans, that is the Amerindians made up 20 per cent of the world's population. Fifty years later, by the middle of the sixteenth century, only 10 million Amerindians remained (Todorov, 1999: 133). Assuming that the population figures for the rest of the world did not vary considerably in those 50 years, then during that period the population of the whole world had been reduced by 17.5 per cent, in other words, out of the 20 per cent Amerindians of the world's population, 50 years into the conquest 2.5 per cent remained. In absolute terms, the population diminution was of the order of 70 million human lives (Todorov, 1999: 133). Before the arrival of the Spaniards, the population of Mexico was about 25 million, in 1532 it had dropped to 17 million, by 1600 it had fallen to 1 million (Parry, 1990: 215f; Todorov, 1999: 133). Different regions, however, were affected differently. The population decline in the coastal regions was much more dramatic than on the plateau. As we have seen in Oviedo's report on working conditions, on many of the Carribbean islands the indigenous population was entirely or almost entirely wiped out, whereas in the coastal regions of Mexico the decline is estimated at about 50 per cent between 1519 and 1532 (Parry, 1990: 216). These figures, however, do not tell us anything about the causes of this demographic catastrophe which are generally held to be, in order of their numerical importance, firstly epidemics which broke out as a result of diseases the Spaniards brought to America and against which the Amerindians had no antibodies; secondly, the change of living conditions for Amerindians as a result of Spanish conquest and rule; and thirdly, outright murders and massacres carried out by the Spaniards (Todorov, 1999: 133).

Although one might be able to make an argument about the cultural significance of diseases, just as one can make an argument about the cultural significance of the spread and distribution of plants and animals as a result of intercultural contact, this chapter will concentrate on the role which cultural assumptions played in directing Spanish political practice in America leading to the massacres and brutalities Las Casas talked about as well as to the destruction of Amerindian cultures and, hence, the destruction of the necessary basis for the survival of the people: ethnocide. Epidemics, although the Spaniards reported on their effects on the Amerindian population and which were clearly responsible for the greatest devastation in terms of numbers, were nevertheless not the object either of the debate or of Spanish policies. There are two reasons for this: on the one hand, epidemics were very common in Europe, too, and taken for granted as a normal feature of human life; on the other hand, unlike subsequently the English in North America, the Spaniards in these early years never deliberately spread diseases among the indigenous population and, hence, did not feel morally responsible for them. I will, therefore, concentrate on the two areas which the Spaniards themselves perceived as deliberate policies based on moral and political considerations, namely the attempts to change Amerindian cultures and the massacres both of which were made possible by the Spanish judgement of Amerindian cultures in relation to their own.

The people who left Spain for America did so for a variety of reasons. Among them were in the beginning explorers, adventurers and sailors. But there were also members of the lower gentry who had fought against the Moors, soldiers of lower rank, artisans, men who fled from Spain either because they had been involved in the *comunero* rebellion or because they were afraid of the Inquisition, such as Jews, *moriscos, conversos*. There were criminals of all kinds who either fled from the authorities or who were actually sent from Spanish prisons to America, cutthroats and lowlives from all walks of life. And then, of course, there were the Franciscan, Dominican, Jeronymite and later Jesuit friars, priests and missionaries (Parry, 1990: 95; 1981: 152). Generally speaking the settlers can be divided into two groups: the friars, priests and missionaries with their interests and motivations on the one hand, and the *conquistadores*, settlers, with a different set of interests on the other.

The great majority of Spaniards who went to America belonged to the latter group. And irrespective of the various reasons they had for leaving Spain, in America they were united by a common goal. They were searching for riches in order to move up the social ladder in Spain, whither they intended to return as fast as possible. What the early voyages had demonstrated quite clearly was that the societies the Spaniards encountered in the Caribbean were not producing luxury goods for trade. Hence, the Spaniards had to fall back onto the two other avenues for becoming rich. Either they would find gold or they would conquer the land and subjugate the people to work it. For their purpose in America it did not matter at all that some of them were farmers and artisans, perfectly capable of making a living; in America they considered themselves soldiers searching for loot and expecting, in so far as they planned to stay in America, to enjoy their rights of conquest and to be supported by the labour of others (Parry, 1990: 100). Consequently, the Spaniards were mainly engaged in two kinds of activity: the search for gold which led to extensive expeditions of exploration, and slave hunting. Indeed, many Spanish expeditions which entered the history books under the term 'war' were nothing else but slave raids (Leed, 1995: 46). These activities, however, were closely connected with each other and both involved interaction with the indigenous population. In the search for gold, the Spaniards needed captives as 'guides, sources of information, interpreters, and leverage over local populations' (1995: 50). Captives also came in handy as compensation for losses, hostages to ensure treaties and 'as a means of quick social advancement, as a source of profit through ransom or sale, as labor' (1995: 50). Captives 'directly ennobled their captors, and when the captives died, their owners lost their social standing, becoming mere peasants' (1995: 55). Women, too, played an important role either as captives or as gifts. For the Spaniards, the gift of women

> signified the acquisition of dependents and their lands, grinders of corn, objects of sexual consumption who elevated the armed vaga-bonds to the status of lord and master. The natives seemed more often to regard the exchange of women as establishing alliances that enjoined obligations of mutual support in the ongoing warfare.
>
> (Leed, 1995: 57)

Wherever the Spaniards succeeded in subjecting whole groups of Amerindians and, thus, in taking control of the land, they divided the land as well as the indigenous population and assigned the latter as permanent servants to individual Spaniards who could employ them any way they liked: the (in)famous *encomienda* system (Parry, 1990: 176).

All these practices were based on and in line with the 'nature' of society, politics, production, 'international relations', as traditionally perceived by the Spaniards. The *encomienda* system had been used in Spain in areas reconquered from the Moors as well as in the Canaries (Parry, 1990: 42). The hierarchical order of society and, in particular, various forms of compulsory labour were all too common in Europe (1990: 175). And so was, of course, the domination of women by men as well as their exchange through marriage in creating bonds between families, gaining lands for a crown or establishing a political bond – one need only recall the political significance for Spain of the marriage between Ferdinand and Isabella. Military expeditions for the purpose of plunder, of making captives or of conquering land and people were common not just in medieval Europe but among many cultures, ancient and contemporary, European and non-European, 'civilized' and 'barbarian' (Leed, 1995: 46).

Cristóbal Colón, again, is a representative example. Although he did describe the peoples he encountered on his voyages occasionally as 'beautiful', 'gentle', 'free from wickedness and unwarlike', very much in line with the traditional understanding of innocent and pure human beings in the original state of nature, these are descriptions in which Colón takes on the role of the observer (Flint, 1992: 136, 144). And yet his interactions with them demonstrate quite clearly that he could not see them as anything else but 'naturally' as servants for the Crown – and this was the best-case scenario for Amerindian converts (1992: 188f). Colón immediately took a 'sample' of Amerindian captives to Spain in order to sell them as slaves; his response to the wild and brutal slave raids his sailors engaged in during Colón's sickness was, when he had recovered, to organize the slave raids properly; and he established *encomiendas* in America (Parry, 1990: 48f; Flint, 1992: 189). The establishment of *encomiendas*, the partition of the indigenous population among the Spanish settlers, was partly forced upon Colón by the rebellion of the Spanish settlers who could not be made to 'clear forests, build houses, and plant crops' but instead roamed the island searching for gold and slaves, living off the food and the women of the Amerindians (Parry, 1990: 48). Hence, the *encomienda* was first introduced in America as an organized means of exploiting and subjecting the indigenous population, replacing the unorganized practices of the settlers in order to ensure some manner of political control. Indeed, the Spanish Crown somewhat later came up against the same kind of pressure with very similar results.

But if all these practices were in accord with older traditions, why should they have had such devastating demographic effects in America? Leaving aside the problem of epidemics, there are two reasons for this catastrophe, both basically leading back to the question of culture. Direct personal violence and massacres were particularly cruel and widespread in America. It appears that the Spaniards' socially and culturally ingrained norms of behaviour – any kind of restraint – simply broke down in what for them was the wilderness. The absence of control through authorities as well as the traditional structures and control of society in combination with the practical demands of slave hunts and explorations seem to have compounded the problem. Small gangs of men were roaming woods teeming with unknown dangers ranging from climate and topography through plants and animals to human beings. They did not know the foodstuffs available, they could not prepare them the usual way, they were not accompanied by women and children, there was no law, no authority, no one to call on and no one to be responsible for. These men knew not, from one hour to the next, from one day to the next, whether they would survive. They suffered 'hunger, exhaustion, nakedness ... all to catch four Indians' or, alternatively, to find gold – sometimes for months on end (Leed, 1995: 44f). In short, nothing in America resembled the known world and the behaviours appropriate for the latter would possibly have led to instant death in the former. The violence and cruelty which grew out of this situation was not only directed towards outsiders, Amerindians, but was also frequently found in the relations among the members of these groups (1995: 26–30).

The second reason for the particularly devastating violence against the Amerindians lay in the place the Amerindian occupied in the worldview of the majority of Spaniards. Bearing in mind that the general justification, as well as for traditional European military expeditions, was the spread of Christianity, the possibility of conversion was decisive for how particular Spaniards acted towards the Amerindians. Most of the settlers agreed whole heartedly with Captain Vargas Machuca's statement that

> these people are by nature barbarians and without any prudence whatsoever, for they are contaminated by barbarian vices of the kind one reads about in the history books. Therefore the war against them is just by natural law, because their nature is such that they cannot be brought to accept Christian doctrine by words. They must be put under the yoke like beasts and compelled with all the rigor of the laws.
>
> (Cf. Hanke, 1974: 136)

All those who believed with Sepúlveda that the 'culture' of the Amerindians had become second nature, that they could not just give up their customs, traditions and way of thinking, argued that violence was necessary to prepare the ground for missionary efforts (Pagden, 1982: 100). For, 'when taught the mysteries of our religion, they [the Amerindians] say that these things might suit Castilians, but not them, and they do not wish to change their customs' (cf. Hanke, 1964: 51). Accordingly, the Dominican Palatino de Curzola argued that 'they will never abandon these evils unless they are first punished and subjected by force and wars, and afterwards preached to' (cf. Hanke, 1974: 125). Furthermore, the Spaniards clearly recognized the 'dangers' of teaching the Christian religion to the Amerindians, for the result might easily have been that 'they have the appearance of Christians, but while they easily receive baptism, with difficulty do they keep to the things promised in it' (cf. Hanke, 1974: 128).[1] Their own pre-existing customs and religion, where they were acknowledged to exist, also implied the dangers of syncretism, so that the Spaniards engaged widely in the systematic destruction of cultural and religious artifacts, including the writings of the Aztecs, for fear of the devil. Many Spaniards who thought along the lines of Sepúlveda's argument clearly saw themselves as 'champions of civilisation and religion against a cruel and superstitious barbarism' (Parry, 1990: 146). Among them the majority of priests, friars and missionaries, including Las Casas' mentor Betanzos, clearly did not believe that the Amerindians were reasonable enough to be left to their own devices (1990: 166). In addition, Sepúlveda argued that 'the loss of a single soul dead without baptism exceeds in gravity the death of countless victims, even were they innocent' (cf. Todorov, 1999: 155). Although it might not be an explanation and is certainly not put forward here as the only cause, without this cultural background we cannot even begin to understand the brutalities the Spaniards committed in America on an extraordinary scale.

For several centuries Las Casas' report on the brutalities of the Spaniards was rejected as biased and exaggerated. Now, however, it is generally accepted as surprisingly accurate not only with respect to the figures Las Casas gives but also with respect to the particular cruelties he described (Todorov, 1999: 132; Bitterli, 1982: 136; Parry, 1990: 143, 145f). Todorov, however, has taken a number of examples from other Spanish reports and I will recount some of them to illustrate the form which direct physical violence took in America. This is not just important as an attempt to take seriously the individual horror and suffering involved, but also because it helps us understand, to some extent at least, what it was that demoralized the Amerindians in such a way that they quite frequently gave up their community life, left old and sick people behind, aborted their babies, fled into the woods and mountains, and committed suicide, sometimes individually, sometimes whole villages (Hanke, 1964: 68).

Thousands of Amerindian lives were lost in what might be described as more or less regular 'wars', like Cortés' conquest of Mexico, or massacres committed in their wake, like the killing of the inhabitants of Tenochtitlan who had gathered in a closed courtyard to celebrate a religious festival. Apart from these killings, however, the Spaniards had trained their dogs to attack Amerindians and quite frequently fed them with living babies ripped from the breasts of their mothers. Crying Amerindian babies were hurled against rocks or into the jungle to stop the noise. The Spaniards bound Amerindian husbands under the bed on top of which they raped the latter's wives. Amerindian workers were not fed properly and frequently died of starvation, as in the case of 800 people on transport from one location to another of whom 600 died. Spaniards tested the sharpness of their swords by ripping open the bellies of the inhabitants of a whole village – men, women, children, old and sick people – for no reason; they ordered forty people at once to be torn apart by Spanish dogs, and cut off the legs, arms and heads of the six hundred inhabitants of a whole village. They hanged the women on trees and bound their babies to their feet, cut off the heads of people on transport if they were not fast enough, and regularly stabbed children to death who would otherwise hold up the party. Should the water for the irrigation of fields run out, they announced, the fields would have to be irrigated with the blood of the Amerindians (Todorov, 1999: 139–42; Bitterli, 1982: 130–6; Stannard, 1992).

These wars, slave hunts and cruelties were regular occurrences and had a devastating effect on the morale of the Amerindians. Much more important for the demographic catastrophe, though, was the systematic destruction of the Amerindian cultures and the introduction of elements of Spanish culture into the natural and social world of America. In the mines and on the Spanish farms, the working conditions were so bad that many Amerindians died of exhaustion and starvation, and the tribute payments demanded of them were so high that they often had to sell all their belongings including their children to money-lenders. Intercourse between men and women was greatly reduced, on the one hand because people were simply too exhausted, and on the other because the men were taken to the mines where they had to stay nine months without any contact with their wives. Under these conditions, the women's health deteriorated to such an extent that, if they got pregnant in the first place, they either miscarried or did not have any milk for their babies after birth. Out of desperation, many aborted the babies or drowned them after birth (Todorov, 1999: 134). The production of food, or rather the impossibility of it, created a vicious circle. Wars, slave hunts and massacres disturbed the regular agricultural activities. Armies destroyed the fields, while people who were brought to the mines or fled from the slave hunters could not engage in food production any more. As a result, the Spaniards who were totally dependent on Amerindian food production, worked their slaves even harder and, hence, even more of them died (Parry, 1990: 173). Fertile land was abandoned and goats, cattle and sheep, introduced by the Spaniards, regularly trampled down the fields of the Amerindians who kept complaining without any effect and often, eventually, gave up farming. In addition, these animals were responsible for soil exhaustion, erosion and, hence, depopulation. The diet of the Amerindians was dramatically affected because they could not afford meat, did not care for milk, but were also prevented from growing their traditional food-stuffs. The effect was 'a wholesale substitution of an animal for a human population' (1990: 218, 218–28). And, thus, we come full circle, for the famished Amerindian population was clearly much more likely to fall prey to the frequent epidemics. Thus, the introduction of Spanish modes of production and of Spanish food, all considered to be in accordance with natural law and, therefore, universally valid, as we have seen above, played a crucial role in the destruction of Amerindian cultures and the diminution of the people.

The brutalities committed by the Spanish settlers as well as the extraordinary death rate of the Amerindians due to the horrendous working conditions triggered a passionate struggle by a number of religious men for the protection of the Amerindians. For the interests of this second group of Spaniards, the friars and missionaries, were seriously threatened by these developments. Many religious men believed that the discovery of America was a positive sign by God. Disappointed with the decadent and sinful life in Europe and the divisions within the Church, they came to America believing that God had placed millions of pagans on this new continent for the Spaniards to discover and convert to Christianity – as a prelude to the conversion of the whole of humankind and, hence, to the end of the world and the beginning of salvation. In America, they believed, they could start building proper Christian communities with the innocent and pure Amerindians, who were not yet as degenerate as the Europeans had become (Erdheim, 1982: 62). But the vision of these Christian orders of building a new, unitary Christian *oikumene* in America could certainly not be realized under these conditions (Cro, 1994: 405f; Hanke, 1974: 5f). The extraordinary death rate of the Amerindians was wiping out the very human material with which these new communities were to be built. In addition, the *encomienda* system neither allowed the friars much access to those Amerindians who were still alive, nor did the latter have any time or energy to listen to the teachings of the missionaries and friars or to attend mass.

Hence, the friars organized opposition to this system and started to put pressure on the Crown, thus endangering the interests of the *conquistadores* and *encomenderos* who, as a result, started to lobby for their own interests with the Crown. Both parties, thus, were exerting all the pressure they could onto one another and onto the Crown. But it would be a mistake to think that the Crown itself only reacted to those pressures. Indeed, when Colón in 1495 sent Amerindians to be sold on the slave market of Seville, Queen Isabella stopped this transaction 'because we wish to be informed by civil lawyers, canonists, and theologians whether we may, with a good conscience, sell these Indians or not' (cf. Pagden, 1982: 31). A year later they were taken from their Spanish masters and sent back to the New World. The Crown clearly had an interest in the revenue from the New World but it also aspired to the leading role in the Christian world and, thus, had to assure that its policies were strictly in accordance with the ethico-political principles of Christianity. And since the papal bulls of 1493 had given America to the Spaniards for the express purpose of Christianizing the indigenous population, the Crown needed to be able to justify its American policies in those terms.

Since the late Middle Ages the Spanish Crown had governed its lands through a hierarchy of *juntas*, councils consisting of theologians, lawyers and political advisers who were trained in Roman law at the universities of the country. These lawyers had indeed worked out quite distinct theories of a constitutional state, less absolute than Hobbes' later version and much broader than the traditional medieval understanding of kingship. In these theories, the Crown was curbed in its exercise of power by positive law, custom and natural law. Such councils, then, were repeatedly used to clarify the legal status of the Amerindians and give policy advice (Parry, 1990: 5f.).

Officially, the Crown based its rights of rule in the Americas on the four papal bulls of 1493. But as we have seen earlier, the Pope's universal dominion was itself highly contentious and, in addition, at least as questionable was whether the Amerindians could be construed as enemies of Christianity – like those peoples with whom in mind the doctrine of the Pope's universal dominion was put forward. Furthermore, the papal bulls had made it abundantly clear that the Amerindians were to be considered human beings and that the Spaniards had the right to rule America for the express purpose of converting them to Christianity. In line with this papal declaration, the Spanish Crown reiterated in all its proclamations that the Amerindians were human beings and had to be treated as such (1990: 174). This, however, did not seem possible under the conditions of constant war, slave raids, forced labour, epidemics and starvation. Over time, the Crown and even some *encomenderos* came to see that the extinction of their labour force did in no way further their interests. The Spaniards in America did not work and, hence, the more Amerindians died the less revenue would the Crown draw from the New World and the more difficult it became for the *encomenderos* to make a profit. On the other hand, it was also clear that the rights of the Amerindians could not be too extensive for fear of rebellions and, in addition, the Crown could not afford to disaffect the *encomenderos* altogether for, after all, without them there could also be no colony and no revenue in the New World. These pressures and considerations, then, gave the Crown an independent incentive to sort out the situation in the New World in addition to the moral outrage that Charles V and his advisers later felt in face of the horrors reported from America.

Hence, in 1510 Palacios Rubios of the Council of Castile was asked to draw up the text of the (in)famous *requerimiento*. In the future, military action could only be undertaken after the *requerimiento* had been read to the Amerindians. In it, they were asked to submit peacefully to the Spanish Crown and accept the Christian faith. It was, however, read to the Amerindians in the Spanish language and from such a distance that the reader, generally a friar, would be out of the reach of arrows. Nevertheless, the Spaniards stuck to the rule of reading it faithfully, even, or maybe precisely because, they knew that it could not have any effect on the Amerindians (Parry, 1990: 138).

The struggle of the friars against this system and for the protection of the Amerindians was sparked off in 1511 by the Dominican Antonio de Montesinos who gave a series of sermons in Santo Domingo in which he criticized the *encomienda* system in no uncertain terms and withheld communion to those *encomenderos* who treated their Amerindians particularly badly. This led to an outrage among the Spanish settlers in America, but Montesinos travelled to Spain and succeeded in convincing the Crown of the seriousness of the situation. In traditional fashion, the Crown convened a *junta* in Burgos which was to examine the allegations and propose reforms. The Laws of Burgos were published in 1512. They upheld the *encomienda* system but set some limits to the hours of work, demanded instruction of the workers, and proper food, housing and clothing. However, the Laws of Burgos also emphasized that the Amerindians were, in principle, free. In practice, all those who were Christians and lived a civilized life, that is like the Spaniards, were to be set free. These laws were, however, hardly implemented (Parry, 1990: 177f).

Meanwhile, Bartolomé de Las Casas, who himself had come to America as a Spanish settler and had held his own *repartimiento*, his share of Amerindian workers, had become a Dominican under the influence of the sermons of Montesinos and took up the fight for the Amerindians. As a result of Las Casas' work, in 1516 a group of three Jeronymite friars were sent to America to report on the implementation of the Laws of Burgos. The *encomenderos*, again, were extremely agitated about this mission which, however, did not accomplish much. It succeeded in freeing those Amerindians who 'belonged' to absentee landlords. But the attempt to find 'capable' Amerindians who could be freed and live like Spaniards failed (Parry, 1990: 178). Las Casas immediately started his next experiment by gathering a group of farmers and artisans in Spain whom he took to the New World. There they were supposed to build a village community along the lines of Spain in which they would support themselves by their own work and, thus, convert the Amerindians by the force of example. Once in the New World, the Spaniards, however, did not see why they had to work for their living while all others just went on slave raids. Las Casas was to be disappointed by his Spaniards as well as by the Amerindians, for the former behaved no differently from other Spaniards in the New World and were eventually killed by the latter (Parry, 1990: 179).

Various attempts to curtail the abuses of the *encomienda* system were made during the 1520s and 1530s. In 1537 Vitoria had analysed the title of Spain in America in a very critical fashion in his lectures. In the same year Pope Paul III issued various bulls in which he condemned slavery in the Americas and insisted that the conviction that the Amerindians did not have reason and were therefore not capable of receiving the faith was heretical. The reports of violence and anarchy in the course of the discovery of Peru, too, influenced public opinion and the Crown. In 1542 the Crown announced the so called New Laws with which a serious attack on the *encomienda* system and slavery was made. Women and children were to be freed immediately and only those males who were legal civil slaves, that is those who had taken part in a rebellion and were enslaved as a result of this, could remain in slavery. All official *encomiendas* were to be terminated and those of private individuals would follow suit at the death of their owners (Parry, 1990: 182–4). The settlers, however, together with the Dominicans in the New World, resisted the implementation of these laws again. They were afraid of an Amerindian rebellion and argued that without the *encomienda* the Spanish settlers would either starve to death or abandon the colony. As a result of these petitions a series of decrees were issued in the late 1540s which upheld the abolition of 'natural' slavery and allowed the *encomienda* to continue, except that now the *encomenderos* could demand tribute in the form of agricultural products from the natives but not any longer labour (1990: 185). These were the developments leading up to the debate in Valladolid in 1550/51 in which Las Casas defended the case of the Amerindians, while Sepúlveda essentially argued the case of the *conquistadores*. Although that debate never produced an official consensus, it nevertheless ended with an unofficial one since, as we saw earlier, Sepúlveda's contribution was considered heretical and was not allowed to be published in Spain.

Although the campaign of the missionaries appears at first sight to be truly in the interests of the Amerindians, it was so only with respect to their survival for the purpose of subjecting them to a totalizing project of cultural change (Leed, 1995: 116). The missionaries, including Las Casas, clearly did not just demand the acceptance of the Christian faith from the Amerindians, but also a Spanish way of life. The separation of religion from social life to which we are used today would have been utterly incomprehensible for the Spaniards. Unlike the *conquistadores*, who had argued that the Amerindians would never give up their own customs unless these were driven out of them by force, the missionaries expected, in line with Las Casas' theory that the Amerindians were innocent peoples in the state of nature, that they would take on the Christian teachings as well as the Spanish way of life without force. This expectation was due to the belief that the Amerindians simply did not have any kind of culture which would have to be replaced. They were believed to live without law, authority, religion – with the exception of idolatry which was regarded as the worship of the devil. Their sexual lives were believed to be entirely unregulated, their clothes were not considered clothes, their dwellings not houses. The missionaries believed that they were filling a void and the Amerindians would receive those gifts of civilization with gratitude (Spicer, 1992: 282). Every single aspect of the social life of the native communities which had been tested for signs of reason and found wanting, as we have seen in the previous chapter, was to be transformed.

When in 1516 the Jeronymite friars came to America in order to implement the Laws of Burgos, they had essentially two tasks. Firstly, in accordance with the Laws of Burgos, they had to find Amerindians who were considered *capaces*, capable of living a Christian and civilized way of life and could, thus, be freed under the terms of the Laws of Burgos. Their second task was to establish villages in which those 'capable' Amerindians could live and, hence, they brought a blueprint for these communities. By means of a questionnaire which was distributed among the older and long-standing members of the Spanish community in Hispaniola the friars attempted 'to discover whether any Indians could be found who were capable of living by themselves and to set free all such Indians, as provided for in the Clarification of the Laws of Burgos' (Hanke, 1974: 9). The third of the seven questions the witnesses were asked cut to the heart of the problem:

> Does the witness know, believe, or has he heard it said or observed, that these Indians, especially those of Espanola and women as well as men, are all of such knowledge and capacity that they should be given complete liberty? Would they be able to live *politicamente* as do the Spaniards? Would they know to support themselves by their own efforts, each Indian mining gold or tilling the soil, or maintaining himself by other daily labor? Do they know how to care for what they may acquire by this labor, spending only for necessities, as a Castilian laborer would?
>
> (Cf. Hanke, 1964: 29)

Indios capaces, then, were Amerindians who had taken on the Christian faith and lived exactly like Spaniards, engaging in mining or agriculture and paying their tributes to the king. However, the missionaries could not find any 'capable' Indians. An Amerindian couple would petition to be set free and could prove that they lived *politicamente*, but they lacked the necessary religious education and were sent into an experimental village. Another native could prove that his religious education was perfect, only he lacked the capability to live a civilized life in all other respects. In a third case, the husband of an Amerindian couple was considered to be sufficiently educated in the faith as well as capable of living like a Spaniard, but his wife was considered to be too old to be 're-educated' and, therefore, not to be set free; the husband decided to stay with his wife in slavery (Hanke, 1964: 69f; Parry, 1990: 178).

Nevertheless, some missionaries and liberally minded public officials engaged in various forms of experiments with the Amerindians. The Franciscan Zumarraga who became Bishop of Mexico as well as the lawyer Vasco de Quiroga, Bishop of Michoacan, were admirers of Thomas More's *Utopia* – to which we will return later in this book – and attempted to establish experimental communities with the Amerindians along the lines of that book (Parry, 1990: 160f; Todorov, 1999: 194). And Las Casas supported the blueprint for experimental villages that the Jeronymite friars carried with them. These blueprints essentially guided missionary activities in America for the next 200 years. They all envisaged, ideally, townships with a church, an administration building and a *plaza* at the centre, surrounded by a grid pattern of streets with proper stone or adobe houses. This set up did not, in fact, resemble most towns in Spain but was copied from the settlements the Romans had built there. A *cacique*, the Spanish name for all Amerindian headmen or leaders,

> together with a friar or a priest and an administrator, will rule the town. Should a Castilian or Spaniard wish to marry an Indian female chief or an Indian chief's daughter or heiress, he may do so with the priest's and the administrator's consent. The Spaniard will then become the town *cacique* and enjoy the same rights and privileges as other *caciques*. This way, it is hoped that all *caciques* will soon be Spaniards and our expenditures will be substantially cut down.
>
> (Las Casas, 1971a: 213f)

The *cacique* was supposed to have jurisdiction in his town but he could only punish perpetrators with the consent of the priest. A Spanish administrator would be responsible for several such towns, inspect them, advise the *caciques* and

> see that the Indians live a well-organized life, that each family remains together and works in the mines or is engaged in the raising of crops and cattle and other occupations described below. He will also see that the Indians are not molested or forced to work overtime. ... He will choose three or four Castilians or other Spaniards to assist him in office, bearing weapons if necessary to enforce the law, and will not allow any Indians, not even the *cacique*, to carry arms unless it be for hunting. ... This administrator will cooperate with the priest to see that the Indians dress properly, sleep in beds, take care of their tools and are satisfied with their wives. A husband should not abandon his wife and the wife must be chaste. Should a wife commit adultery and should a husband complain about it, the priest and the administrator must be consulted before the *cacique* punishes both the wife and her lover, since punishment for this does not exceed beating. Indians may not be allowed to exchange, sell or gamble their belongings – except food and charity contributions – without permission from the priest and the administrator, and they must not be allowed to eat on the ground. ... Each town will have a

religious man to instruct the Indians in the Catholic Faith, adminis-
ter the sacraments, preach on Sundays and holidays, explain the tithe
owed to God, the Church and its ministers, act as confessor, bury the
dead and pray for their souls. Indians must be made to attend mass
and to sit in order, men and women separately. . . . those who refuse
to come will receive a mild punishment in public in order to serve as
an example for all. The sexton may be an Indian, provided he be
found capable of assisting in the Mass, teaching children – especially
those of important families – up to nine years of age to read, write
and speak the Castilian tongue, and on the whole also teaching all
adults to speak Castilian.

(Las Casas, 1971a: 214f)

This document further spelled out exactly the hours of work and of
leisure, the number of livestock, the rations of meat for the different
classes of the Amerindians, how the income was to be divided between
the king, the *cacique* and the workers, what exactly the priest had to buy
for the different housholds in terms of clothes, chickens and so on. The
encomenderos were to be recompensed for the loss of their Amerindians
by the king who should provide ships and arms for the attacks on the
Caribs, who were supposed to be cannibals and resisted missionary
efforts and, thus, could be caught as slaves (Las Casas, 1971a: 216ff;
Hanke, 1974: 131).

In the early years, the Spaniards repeatedly tried to set up these
experimental villages. The governor Nicolas de Ovando selected his
best *caciques* and a group of Amerindians to live as expected. As soon
as the Amerindians were left to themselves, they spent their time eating,
drinking and dancing and showed no interest whatsoever in mining
gold. After six years, the friars were told that the Amerindians had
proven beyond any doubt that they could not live a civilized life as
free people (Hanke, 1964: 36f). Against the resistance of the *encomenderos*, Rodrigo de Figueroa had freed three Amerindian villages and come
to the same conclusion. He made one last attempt and gave 16 Amerindians to one of his relatives; they were given food and tools and
brought to the mines where they were expected to mine gold without
the help of the Spaniards. After two months, they had eaten all the food
but had produced hardly any gold (1964: 44ff). In 1526 Francisco de
Guerrero was made responsible for the experimental village in Bayamo
where he was supposed to teach the Christian faith, demonstrate
European agricultural techniques, prevent the Amerindians from
religious ceremonies involving idolatry – the use of the traditional

masks – but allow them their dances. Guerrero visited the village very rarely, used the Amerindians as servants for his household, and invited his friends for a big feast when the Amerindians had brought in a harvest (1964: 61ff). The governor Manuel Rojas found the village in a condition of chaos. Many inhabitants had fled, others died, and the rest were hungry and rebellious (1964: 65ff). All these official experiments led the Spaniards to conclude that the Amerindians were simply not capable of being freed and living a civilized and Christian way of life.

What these experiments aimed at were the wholesale replacement of one culture by another, of one form of production and distribution by another, of one form of religion by another, of one form of gender relations by another, of one form of political organization by another, down to such basics as the introduction of men's trousers (Spicer, 1992: 5, 282). Despite, or rather because of, the insistence of the missionaries that the Amerindians did not have any culture and, therefore, could be taught with non-violent means rather than the violent ones of the *encomienda*, their goal was perfectly in accord with that of the *encomenderos*. Both strategies aimed at nothing less than a full-scale destruction of Amerindian cultures or ways of living. And despite the missionaries' insistence on achieving this end by what Las Casas called 'the methods of Christ', that is non-violence and example, the missionaries did indeed regularly employ violence. On the one hand, they consistently and publicly destroyed 'idols', carved deities, pictures, masks and any artefact which might be used in religious ceremonies, including many which were, of course, not. And they did not stop there but went on to destroy temples and shrines; they systematically hammered stone carvings from the face of buildings. And they engaged in the wholesale and very effective destruction of Amerindian manuscripts, many of which were of a perfectly harmless temporal nature – hardly any of the Aztec rolls have survived (Spicer, 1992: 298; Parry, 1990: 161).

But they also employed – and regularly – violence against human beings. First of all, although the missionaries generally tried to keep 'their' Amerindians separated and out of the reach of Spanish *encomenderos* and Spanish towns because these were sinful places which were thought to have a degenerating influence on the innocent Amerindians, they nevertheless regularly were accompanied by and cooperated with soldiers who often had to ensure the authority of the missionary. And it was not uncommon for a missionary to ask the soldiers to, for instance, behead groups of rebellious Amerindians (Spicer, 1992: 324). The missionaries also set up whipping posts in the villages and punished those Amerindians who, for example, did not come to mass, or who had committed adultery, or who did not work in the prescribed way, with public beatings. Mission discipline was enforced in the harshest way, and even criticized by Spanish courts who had to replace missionaries for fear that their brutality might trigger rebellions as, in fact, it frequently did. Missionaries were known to beat Amerindian perpetrators to death and many of the Amerindian rebellions were preceded by systematic corporal punishments through missionaries (1992: 325).

> We may say that the Spaniards employed force to get the Indians to live according to their legal and political system, to make them work regularly in their economic enterprises, to persuade them to follow the weekly plan of worship in the churches, and to give up aspects of their religion classed by the missionaries as idolatry or worship of the Devil.
>
> (Spicer, 1992: 326)

Thus, if the theoretical debate appeared to offer a backward, violent theory of colonization put forward by Sepúlveda, and a tolerant, liberal, humanist, gentle and loving approach supported by Las Casas, we now have to draw the conclusion that with respect to their outcomes these two approaches did not significantly differ. Furthermore, despite the fact that the two parties, missionaries and *conquistadores*, exerted pressure on the Crown in support of their programmes, from the start, 'Church and civil officials were in agreement' about the elements of civilization the Amerindians had to take on (Spicer, 1992: 282). And we have to draw the conclusion that, in a way, Sepúlveda and his supporters were actually closer to the truth in their conception of the Amerindians as peoples with cultures, and in their judgement that these peoples would not want to give up this culture so easily. This is borne out by the fact that, as Spicer, who has written the most comprehensive and detailed account of the process of acculturation in which he emphasizes the differences between not only the Amerindian communities but also their interactions with the Spaniards and later the Mexicans and the Anglo-Americans, put it: 'Probably the easiest generalization to make which would apply to all the Indians of the region is that all offered resistance and at some time fought to maintain their independence of White domination' (1992: 16). In addition, the non-violence of the missionary theory was entirely dependent and built on the assumption that the Amerindians did not have culture but the potential for reason and would, therefore, take on the reasonable Spanish culture without any resistance. As soon, however, as masks, for instance, turned up in the Amerindian communities and, thus, suggested that there was something like culture, this triggered immediate violent destruction at the hands of the missionaries. And, likewise, as soon as the missionaries encountered resistance to their teachings from the Amerindians, indicating that either the Amerindians did not have the reason expected or that they were driven by alternative cultural norms, violence again was the response of choice for the missionaries.

What is important for the following part of this study, however, is that the concept of the state of nature and its supposed embodiment in Amerindian peoples continued to play an immensely important role in Europe. First of all, Las Casas' writings – and among them *The Devastation of the Indies*, in which he described the atrocities committed against the innocent Amerindians in the New World – were widely translated and widely read, in particular in combination with De Bry's engravings depicting those same massacres. The book came out in the Netherlands and in Germany in Latin, it was translated into English, and served in particular in Protestant countries as anti-Spanish propaganda (Parry, 1990: 143). Hence, Las Casas' constant argument that the Amerindians were indeed human beings in the state of nature had found a widespread audience. And, it should be mentioned, since the concept of the state of nature and an innocent state of mankind in its religious form was already part and parcel of the Christian worldview, it was not difficult to imagine that an equivalent secular concept might without much resistance be taken up. In addition, it is interesting to see that the missionaries in the New World two hundred years and many, many disappointments later were still operating on the principle that the Amerindians were people in the state of nature, that they did not have any kind of culture. The Jesuit Adam Gilg wrote in 1692:

> They live without God, without faith, without Princes, and without houses...they have none of those coarse vices...neither idolatry nor magic nor drunkenness nor avarice nor the abuse of having a number of wives at the same time nor lewdness are in vogue among them. The whole time that I have been living among these otherwise half-bestial people, I have not heard that an unmarried woman has been seduced, although the silly thing (since almost everyone goes naked) must mightily incite them to it.
>
> (Cf. Spicer, 1992: 313)

The missionaries by this time had been disappointed many times over. In the beginning they had been successful in getting 'their' Indians exempted from tribute payments for ten years after which time, they were convinced, they would have Christianized and civilized all of them. This expectation did not come true and they were forced to negotiate for extensions of the period of exemption over and over again (Spicer, 1992: 292f). Even in the early years of Spanish colonization, the missionary programme, staffed and executed by an extremely well disciplined, motivated and organized elite of missionaries, did not bear the expected fruits. After the middle of the sixteenth century, the men of the Church had largely lost their belief in the wholesale conversion of the American pagans (Parry, 1990: 164f). And they had had to confront the fact that, as with other cultural areas, they could be successful in destroying culture and religion in its traditional form; they might even be successful in getting some rituals, prayers or feasts integrated into Amerindian life; but that did not mean that the Amerindians had become Christians. The two religions might live side by side in a community; they might merge, and only the formal rituals of one of them, Christianity, might survive but with its meaning changed. Notwithstanding all these experiences, the missionaries, two hundred years after the discovery, were still working on the assumption of an innocent state of nature. And so were classical European thinkers, as we will see in Part II of this study.

Part II

The State of Nature and the Reconstitution of European Thought

5
The Tyranny of the European Context: Reading Classical Political Theory in International Relations

'What was it which gave unity to the ideas about the structure and development of society generated in Europe during ... the century traditionally described as the Enlightenment?' (Meek, 1976: 1). Against the deeply held beliefs of (almost all) European scholars I will argue in the following pages that the answer to this question is: the discovery of the American Indian. The 'discovery' of 'natural man', or rather the identification of the American Indian with man in the state of nature, triggered a revolution in, or perhaps even the emergence of what would later become, the modern social sciences. In the first instance, now that 'natural man' had been 'discovered' one could 'apply to the study of man and society those "scientific" methods of enquiry which had recently proved their worth and importance in the sphere of natural science' (1976: 1). Secondly, the identification of the American Indian with man in the state of nature led to a redefinition of history along a linear timescale providing a secular *telos* as the basis of the historical process (Lestringant, 1994: 174; Cro, 1994: 388f; Pagden, 1993: 93, 111, 115). Thirdly, the 'discovery' of man in the state of nature provided European reformers with a basis from which to criticize the particular historical development of their own societies and with the means to theoretically reconstruct an alternative, universally valid, political community. Taken together, these three levels – epistemological, ontological and ethical – amount to a total redefinition of authentic and legitimate political community – a definition which, for example, in the French Revolution and in the constitution of the North American society became the guiding principle for political practice. At the same time, however, the theoretical construction of a universal linear timescale and

95

a political community built on universal natural law inevitably led to a ranking of all human societies on that linear scale. Thus, paradoxically, the universalist conception of the state of nature brought with it a worldview based on a hierarchy of cultures which served as the basis for a theory of unequal relations between political communities.

I will substantiate these claims in the next chapter. However, since these claims as well as my approach to classical political theory are in many ways unfamiliar and provide scope for misunderstandings I will attempt, in this chapter, to clarify the precise status of the argument. Conventional readings of classical political and social thought differ in two major respects from my own approach. Firstly, conventional interpretations of classical thought tend to be 'Eurocentric'. This in the sense that the canon of texts worthy of interpretation is restricted to European authors; their contextualization tends to concentrate almost entirely on European political and historical events; and their integration into a history of ideas also tends to be constructed as an exclusively European one. That is, we are confronted with an entirely self-referential interpretation of European authors by European authors which, despite the rich insights it no doubt has produced, tends to seriously underestimate even the potential impact from and meaning for the relationship between Europeans and non-Europeans. I will demonstrate the limitations of this approach in the first part of this chapter. In the second part of this chapter I will show that there is, however, another more serious problem in conventional interpretations of classical social and political thought, namely that contemporary thinkers share with their classical counterparts a particular definition of knowledge. By that I mean that the concept of the state of nature in its separation from and opposition to culture underpins the separation of theory and practice in both classical and modern social thought. As a result, modern interpretations of classical thinkers tend to overlook the concrete historical and political contents of the latter's theories.

Unlike conventional interpretations, then, what I intend to show in the next chapter is the cultural unity and particularism of European political thought, domestic and international. And this cultural unity, in its modern form, I will argue, is to a great extent influenced by the discovery of America and the assumptions made about the American Indians. This argument seems to contradict the fact that

the classical texts in political theory and the majority of commentaries on those texts tend to concentrate heavily upon the construction and maintenance of internal order. The main focus of political theory tends to be the theory of the state and not interstate theory.

(Williams, 1996: 143)

This is undoubtedly true. Hobbes's *Leviathan*, Locke's *Two Treatises of Government* or Rousseau's *Social Contract* are all attempts to theoretically construct a viable and good internal order. And only after these domestic theories have been worked out, and on their basis, does the international then come into play. At the end of the *Social Contract* Rousseau wrote:

> Now that I have laid down the true principles of political right, and tried to give the State a basis of its own to rest on, I ought next to strengthen it by its external relations, which would include the law of nations, commerce, the right of war and conquest, public right, leagues, negotiations, treaties, etc. But all this forms a new subject that is far too vast for my narrow scope. I ought throughout to have kept to a more limited sphere.

(Rousseau, 1993: 309)

Rousseau's famous statement is symptomatic for European political thought in two ways. Like Rousseau, although they have commented on international issues here and there, most political philosophers never provided a systematic treatment of the international. And, more importantly, like Rousseau they took the domestic as an indispensable basis for any thought on the international. There is a clear direction to political thought, from the domestic to the international, from inside to outside, from France (or Germany, or Britain, or Spain) to Europe and from there to the rest of the world. I am going to argue, however, that there is another, an unreflected, flow of ideas and events from the international to the domestic, a reverse undercurrent which can clearly be shown in the writings of the classical authors. But if this reverse current is so obvious, so easy to demonstrate, why has it not been taken up and discussed before?[1] The first reason for this neglect is the established ways of reading and interpreting classical political theory which, at the very least, make it very difficult to maintain a systematically global perspective. The second, and much deeper, reason is that we share with the classical authors, consciously or unconsciously, a definition of social theory on the basis of which we conduct our analyses. And these shared assumptions prevent us frequently from inquiring into the processes of their own emergence and development; we simply take them for granted and, oftentimes, read them back into history.

Conventionally, commentators first of all take the pronounced intentions of classical political thinkers seriously and interpret their writings, quite legitimately, in the light of these intentions. In order to broaden or deepen the analysis, commentators traditionally have the choice among a range of options. Either they try to locate a particular author in a tradition of thought: they construct a history of ideas, which at its extreme generally goes back to ancient Greek philosophers and extends to contemporary writers. This strategy often entails very diligent comparisons of the positions and arguments by different authors on a particular topic in which their commonalities and differences are worked out in detail. Or they seek to interpret the work of a classical thinker in the context of his time, that is in terms of what the particular problems were that he personally or his society generally experienced as requiring a solution. And, of course, these two approaches can be, and frequently are, combined. Notwithstanding the deep insights that these established modes of interpreting classical political theory produce, they all overlook the importance of the international for the domestic. That this is true not only for political theory narrowly defined, but also, and more importantly, for those authors whose explicit purpose it is to analyse the relevance of political thought for international relations, will be shown in the following pages.

Howard Williams, for instance, states explicitly that traditional political theory which dealt with the relationship between the individual and the state with the domestic 'may have its limitations' and argues that 'the gap between international relations and political theory needs to be bridged' (Williams, 1996: 146). This need arises out of a 'genuine novelty' in historical development, namely 'the globalization of human life'; the times have changed and, thus, 'political theory...has to change with the times' (1996: 145f). This does not necessarily mean, though, that classical political theory has become outdated. On the contrary, Williams suggests that international relations and political theory 'are not on closer inspection such remote intellectual preoccupations' and that 'many political thinkers have earlier pointed out that some of the bases of human society were transforming in a transnational direction' (1996: 147, 141). What we need to do, then, is to reread the classical authors, paying closer attention to those aspects of their arguments which might pertain to a transnational, interdependent or global society. This discovery, that classical political theory might after all, despite its preoccupation with the domestic, have something to say about the international, is shared by Torbjørn Knutsen. He disputes the observation that 'speculation about the state goes back to antiquity whereas speculation about the relations between states goes back little further than to World War I' (Knutsen, 1992: 1). On the contrary, he argues that 'scholars, soldiers and statesmen have, in fact, speculated about the relations between states since the modern state emerged four or five centuries ago' (1992: 1). This is clearly also the opinion of David Boucher who intends to 'retrieve the intellectual heritage of the political theory of international relations on the assumption that its severance from international theory in the twentieth century has been contingent and accidental rather than logical and necessary' and who, in addition, argues that one cannot understand the narrower international issues the classical thinkers discussed 'by detaching (them) from the rest' (Boucher, 1998: 11). Thus, 'when we look, for example, at theories which justify or condemn the colonization of the Americas . . . they are hardly intelligible unless we identify the theory of property which informs the discussion' (1998: 11).

One way or another, these three authors start from the same assumption and share the same goal. They start from the assumption that we can learn something about international relations from classical political theory, and they want to demonstrate the close interconnection between these two disciplines. But how do they go about their projects? First of all, there is a choice of authors – one is almost tempted to say a canon of authoritative texts much like that which the Spaniards had. Prominent among those classical authors whose writings are illuminating the interface between domestic and international politics are Machiavelli, Hobbes, Vitoria, Grotius, Pufendorf, Locke, Vattel, Kant, Rousseau. One aspect which these authors have in common is that they are all European thinkers. There is, of course, nothing wrong with studying European political thought. After all, it is exactly what I intend to do in the next chapter, covering most of the same authors. Nevertheless, it needs to be pointed out that the analysis of European authors by European authors is, in cultural terms, self-referential. That is, if there is a cultural unity and particularism embedded in European political thought, then this approach will certainly not uncover it.

Secondly, both Boucher and Knutsen place the respective authors to some extent into the context of a history of ideas. Thus, for Knutsen there are 'Preludes' to the modern age to which the above-mentioned authors belong. These preludes deal with medieval and ancient Greek authors (Knutsen, 1992: chs 1, 2). And despite the fact that Boucher explicitly presents the classical theorists in a thematic rather than a chronological fashion, he, too, presents ancient Greece and Thucydides as the forerunners of 'Empirical Realism' and the Greeks, Stoics and medieval authors like Aquinas as the forerunners of the 'Universal Moral Orders' theorists (Boucher, 1998: 12, chs 3, 4, 8, 9). These predecessors of the classical authors, then, are Europeans, too.

Thirdly, the analysis often proceeds by way of comparing the position and argument of one European author with one or several others. Williams, for instance, compares Hegel's and Kant's writings on world history with each other (Williams, 1996: ch. 8). Boucher sets out Vitoria's and Gentili's positions on the justice of war and compares them with the medieval thought of Augustine and Aquinas (Boucher, 1998: 200–3), but his thematic order of the authors in the first place does, of course, set up different categories, different schools of thought as alternative and comparable ways of thinking about politics, domestic and international. And Knutsen arranges, for instance, Kant versus 'many Atlantic authors' (Knutsen, 1992: 111).

All that was said in the previous three paragraphs is, of course, not meant to be a criticism of the comparative method, the analysis of a history of ideas or the study of European political thought. The examples I have given were in no way systematic but randomly picked. The object of this exercise was simply to demonstrate on a very superficial level that these conventional methods of reading and analysing and depicting classical political thinkers actually construct a universe in the mind of the reader: a universe gradually peopled by more and more thinkers; a universe with a long and impressive – and often also cumulative – history; a universe, nevertheless, in which differences of opinion abound, alternative approaches and positions on various political issues are aired and fought over. The richer in people and thoughts and developments this universe becomes, the deeper we dive into the intricacies of thought and debate, the more we lose sight of the fact that the representation of the rest of the world by these authors might not be generally valid or depict the outer limits of what is thinkable about the world.

This problem might, however, be solved at least partly by the historical and social contextualization in which Boucher, Knutsen and Williams also engage or for which they at least call. Knutsen, for instance, focuses his attention on the interaction between modern states on the one hand and the theory of sovereignty on the other, both of which are, he says, 'intimately intertwined through modern history' (Knutsen, 1992: 2). Consequently, at the beginning of each chapter he provides a summary of the historical and social developments and problems with which the classical authors dealt in their theories and in which those theories have to be understood and located.

Similarly, Boucher maintains that 'events have a place in this book in so far as they set the problems which the philosophers address', and he, too, frequently provides summaries of those events (Boucher, 1998: 12). Meanwhile, Williams clearly calls for the rereading of the classical authors in light of 'what happened to politics in the twentieth century', that is although he does not necessarily place them in their own time, he does propose to analyse them with the problems of a particular, the contemporary, time in mind (Williams, 1996: 141). Clearly, this kind of historical context should allow us to relativize not only in temporal but also in spatial terms the position of our classical thinkers in their universe. In temporal terms, the clarification of the historical context might tell us that, however much a theory was formulated in general terms, it was a particular problem the theorist had in mind when discussing it. Bearing in mind that we are confronted with theories attempting to bridge the domestic and the international, to analyse the interface between those two areas of thought, the introduction of international conflicts might be expected to relativize the pantheon of European authors in spatial terms.

Let us take a closer look at Knutsen's introduction to the modern world, then. 'The emergence of the modern world can be captured through analysis of three key inventions which appeared in Western Europe in the long sixteenth century: fire arms, the compass and the printing press' (Knutsen, 1992: 43). Although there is no question that firearms, the compass, and the printing press were very important inventions, they tell us nothing about who could be shot and under what conditions with those firearms, which goals one wanted to reach with the compass, and what kinds of texts were printed and distributed. Indeed, Knutsen goes on to discuss various intra-European developments in the sixteenth century with particular emphasis on the divisions in the Church and the Reformation (1992: 44–8). In this latter context, Knutsen introduces Francisco de Vitoria and Gentili. Vitoria, he tells us, 'was among the first Spanish jurists to warn against the dangers of making religion a cause for war' (Knutsen, 1992: 50). In Knutsen's version, Vitoria's lecture on just war and religion has apparently nothing to do with the discovery of America and the legal and moral problems of justifying the Spanish 'wars' against peoples who were neither Christian nor enemies of Christianity. For Knutsen, this lecture is only relevant in the context of the European Reformation.

However, a few pages later, Knutsen returns to Vitoria, now in the context of the discovery of the New World. He tells us that between 1492 and 1515 the Spanish activities in the New World consisted of 'coastal expeditions'; after the following '25 years of intense effort, the great age of the *conquista* was over' (1992: 52). There is no mention of the indigenous population on the Caribbean islands which had been systematically enslaved and, on many islands, wiped out in those years of 'coastal expeditions', and the 'great age of the *conquista*' comprises only the conquest of the Aztec Empire and the destruction of the Inca Empire. To be sure, Knutsen does report on the famous debate between Las Casas and Sepúlveda, and he discusses Vitoria's lectures on the American Indians. Since, in his historical summary, he did not actually mention those native Americans who lived outside the Aztec and the Inca empires and who were, by Las Casas and others, identified with human beings in the state of nature, it does not come as a surprise that Knutsen misses the relevance of the debate on the 'nature' of the Amerindians. The debate between Las Casas and Sepúlveda was triggered by the 'unspeakable cruelties' which the settlers committed against the Amerindians and, according to Knutsen, Sepúlveda and others defended those with 'legal and religious sophisms' while Las Casas 'gained fame as an indefatigable champion of the rights of the Indians' (Knutsen, 1992: 52). What these rights were or why they should have been problematic to establish in the first place, we are not told. Nor are we told anything about the extensive discussion on the nature of the Amerindians in Vitoria's work, the very work which Knutsen cites. Although Knutsen discusses Vitoria's arguments about the lack of Christianity as not sufficient a reason to deny pagans their property rights or lead wars against them, he does not explain why this discussion should have taken place in this context and not with respect to other pagans Europeans had encountered before in other parts of the world (1992: 53).

Knutsen summarizes:

> Vitoria's defence of the Indians is, in some ways, quite modern; for example, his discussion includes assertions of the right to private property, to travel and trade. In other aspects, the treatise is rife with medieval concerns; the discussions of war and peace, for example, rely on Aristotle, Augustine and Aquinas and their assumptions on divine, natural law. Vitoria's view on politics was dominated by individual decisionmakers, by princes and soldiers, the choices they faced and by the nature and the moral and legal implications of their acts.
>
> (Knutsen, 1992: 55)

Knutsen's interest is entirely governed by intra-European developments; rights of property, trade and travel are modern in European eyes;

Aristotle, Augustine and Aquinas are medieval European thinkers. But there is more to learn here. For instance, why and since when are property, trade and travel modern since people have engaged in these activities for a thousand years or so before the 'modern age'? Could it be that their theoretical reinterpretation *in the context of the discovery of America* catapulted them from the medieval into the modern age, for instance?

Hence, in Knutsen's case the historical contextualization does not widen our horizon, rather it seems to confirm and strengthen our Euro-centric propensities. But we have to be careful with our criticism, for Knutsen states right at the beginning that he intends, for the purposes of this book, to define International Relations theory rather narrowly as dealing with 'interactions between sovereign states' and since the sovereign states 'emerged out of the tumultuous interaction in Western Europe' he will focus on 'Western events' and 'European theorists' (1992: 2), which might explain why the Aztec and Inca Empires play a role but the 'natural men' do not. In any case, his approach is perfectly legitimate and logical so long as one can assume that extra-European events have had no impact on the development of the state. And Knutsen does just that. He takes the modern state to be a European phenomenon – which no doubt it is – and reads that phenomenon back into literature dating from *before* its emergence. But, as we shall see in the next chapter, for the emergence and development of the European sovereign state, at least in the eyes of some of its major theoreticians, extra-European events were quite important and, in addition, I hope to show that what influenced the development of classical political thought most strongly were precisely *not* state-like entities like the Aztec or the Inca Empires, but those political communities which were perceived as not having built states at all.

Knutsen, I believe, does not stand alone. The power of the Europeans over non-European peoples, ever since the discovery of America, the all too obvious influence of European thought, European institutions, European practices on non-European peoples all over the world, in addition to the conventional strategies of reading political theory mentioned above, all of these make it difficult even to imagine that the interaction between Europeans and non-Europeans might have had an important and lasting impact not just on those powerless non-Europeans but also on European development itself. Nevertheless, 'natural man' is built into the very foundations of our political and international theories. Indeed, 'natural man' is the reason for the division between these two disciplines. While the former constructs domestic theories of the good life on the basis of principles derived from 'natural man', the latter justifies the non-extension of equal rights to those societies who do not seem to live up to these domestic European ideals. But while most scholars would probably agree in theory with Williams' statement that, at least in some sense, 'just as individuals are unavoidably social beings so now states are almost necessarily both national and international entities' (Williams, 1996: 142), it seems more difficult to take the assumption that systematic interaction between states or political communities must have some impact on both parties, not just on one of them, serious in practice. And this difficulty has wide-ranging implications, not only for Knutsen who simply does not even consider the possibility that the systematic interaction with the native Americans might also have had some repercussions for the Spaniards beyond a greater revenue or the need to defend their American holdings against the colonial aspirations of other European powers.

Williams himself, for instance, encounters this problem, too, albeit in a different way. For he repeatedly argues that states are 'social beings' only 'now', in the twentieth century (1996: viii, 141, 142, 145, 156, 157). And it is under the guidance of these new developments of the contemporary world that he rereads Locke, Kant, Grotius and others. Thus, Williams does not analyse the international historical context and accepts to quite a great extent that the classical authors focused on the domestic rather than the international (1996: 143). In approaching classical authors with a twentieth-century problem in mind, Williams does, of course, run quite a risk. For without an analysis of the historical context, domestic and international, the concrete meanings of theoretical statements might not reveal themselves. But, more importantly, the political and normative contents of those classical theories might be carried in an entirely unexamined way into the twentieth century. Such is the case, for instance, in Williams' discussion of Locke. The 'economically aggressive side of Locke's theory', that is the introduction of exclusive property rights and the exploitation of natural resources, states Williams, 'has led to criticism' (Williams, 1996: 106). Against this criticism Williams defends Locke with the argument that his theory was also responsible for positive developments such as

> the spread of a liberal political culture throughout the world and an economic system which led to much higher standards of life. The commercial spirit which goes hand in hand with Locke's political theory led to improved communications and undermined other, less equal social relations. Quite often traditional societies were largely stagnant and, in many instances, barbaric. The least that can be

said of Locke's theory is that its adoption created new and, for some, unimagined opportunities.

(Williams, 1996: 106)

Williams simply accepts that traditional societies were stagnant and/or barbaric compared with the progressive and liberal character of what Locke proposed, overlooking that Locke, on the one hand, derived his liberal principles from a conception of the state of nature backed up with countless examples taken from these 'barbaric' Amerindian societies while, on the other, deliberately providing a justification for the expropriation of these same 'barbaric' societies for the proprietors of the Carolina Company. Much more important than that, however, is the fact that while Williams here defends a theory of colonization and the accompanying practice, which for many of the colonized peoples did not open up any opportunities but ended them, often enough together with their lives, he then goes on to accept what he regards as a valid critique of Locke, namely that over-exploitation, not of people but of the globe, and over-population 'in the contemporary global context ... are maybe strong grounds to reconsider the applicability of Locke's expansionist theory' (Williams, 1996: 107). The problem with this approach, then, is that those elements of a classical theory which seem to pertain to a contemporary problem, in this case the ecological problem, are acknowledged much more clearly and weighed much more heavily than those elements which seem to only have been important in the past. Thus, colonization and, in particular, the suffering of indigenous 'barbaric' nations under what amounted at times clearly to genocidal practices is not just downplayed against the contemporary ecological problem; indeed, this approach overlooks the fact that, first of all, the negative effects of colonization on the one hand and the positive propagation of a liberal political culture on the other are not just coexisting in Locke's theory but mutually constitutive as well as constitutive of the theory itself. And for this reason, the defence of Locke's liberal political culture does not just do injustice to those who have suffered in the past but it also – inadvertently to be sure – justifies the negative constitutive element of this theory for the contemporary world. Is it a coincidence that, again, nature, that is the contemporary ecological crisis, is held up against culture, the backward, stagnant barbarians?

Let us look ahead, then, to my argument that the American Indians were, indeed, crucial for the modern understanding of the state of nature and for the construction of natural law on its basis. David

Boucher, who is clearly much more perceptive in reading the classical authors than Knutsen is, discusses the centrality of the concept of the state of nature in several classical theories, so for example in his treatment of Pufendorf and Hobbes (Boucher, 1998: 223–9, 246–50, 149–63). He is also very aware of the relevance of these discussions for the justification of conquest in America in particular and colonialism in general. Nevertheless, he, too, does not see that the American Indian plays a rather special role in the construction of the state of nature. I will use Boucher's discussion of Hobbes as an example.

First of all, Boucher quite rightly stresses the point that Hobbes – but also Pufendorf, Rousseau and others – after elaborating the characteristics of the state of nature did not believe that this 'ideal type' state of nature – the war of every man against every man – has ever existed historically throughout the world (Boucher, 1998: 145; Hobbes, 1997: 89). However, in the same sentence in which he declares that this state of nature has never really existed as a concrete historical condition, Hobbes does point to the Amerindian communities as evidence for the plausibility of his logical deduction of the state of nature:

> It may peradventure be thought, there was never such a time, nor condition of warre as this; and I believe it was never generally so, over all the world: but there are many places, where they live so now. For the savage people in many places of *America*, except the government of small Families, the concord whereof dependeth on naturall lust, have no government at all; and live at this day in that brutish manner, as I said before.
>
> (Hobbes, 1997: 89)

Boucher picks up on this contradiction and suggests that there are actually two different concepts of the state of nature to be found in Hobbes, namely a 'hypothetical, or logical, state of nature and the historical, pre-civil condition' which he also calls the 'modified state of nature' (Boucher, 1998: 149, 157). But why, Boucher asks, does Hobbes feel the need to come up with this second, modified state of nature, for which he can present historical evidence and of which he truly believed that it had existed as a concrete historical condition 'in pre-civil times' (1998: 149)? The answer is that Hobbes needed precisely that historical evidence because he defined the social sciences along the lines of the natural sciences, that is dependent on empirical evidence (1998: 149). And Boucher goes on to argue that for Hobbes the 'relations among states are *not* very like relations among individuals in the mere state of nature. Instead relations among states can more fruitfully be seen as analogous to a modified...stage of the hypothetical state of nature, and the historical pre-civil condition' (1998: 149).

In fact, Boucher makes two points here which I will make with respect to all the classical authors I am going to deal with in the following pages. Firstly, he maintains that Hobbes' understanding of the natural and social sciences necessitates empirical evidence. Hence, the empirical evidence of the Amerindian communities to which Hobbes points is crucially important for the plausibility of his logical deduction of a hypothetical state of nature. Secondly, Boucher clearly argues that Hobbes' analogy for the state of nature between states, i.e. the international state of nature, is precisely *not* the *hypothetical* state of nature but that real existing concrete historical condition in pre-civil times for which the Amerindian communities are Hobbes' contemporary example/evidence. If I, in dealing with classical political theory in the following pages, stress the importance of the Amerindians I do not question at any point the fact that many of the classical authors maintain that the state of nature is just a theoretical device. What I do argue instead is that the empirical evidence presented in all these cases is taken from the Amerindians and that this evidence is crucially important precisely because the social sciences were understood along the lines of the natural sciences. In addition, I am not suggesting that all the authors I am going to mention share one and the same theoretical understanding of the state of nature. Indeed, in most cases their writings were at least partly motivated by their disagreements on this issue; thus Rousseau, for instance, in the *Essay on the Origins of Inequality* launches a scathing critique not only of Hobbes' understanding of the state of nature in particular, but also of those of Locke and Pufendorf. At one level, as I will argue in the next chapter, these differences are important; at another level, however, it is precisely the common procedure to provide evidence taken from the Amerindian societies which is decisive for my argument.

This leads me to the second point of contention, namely the claim that the most important sources for the classical writers generally were the Greek and Roman classics and, in particular, that examples for the state of nature have been provided by these writers of antiquity, were used by authors like Hobbes and, hence, the examples of the Amerindians were not only not particularly important but could even have been dispensable. Again, Boucher can be used as an example since he maintains that Hobbes in general 'relies heavily upon Thucydides'

(Boucher, 1998: 149), and in providing evidence for that historical 'pre-civil' state in particular makes reference to a number of communities such as 'the Amazon women, Saxon and other German families, the American Indians, and the paternal communities of Ancient Greece' (1998: 157). And, indeed, this list appears to suggest that the absence or presence of the Amerindians in particular would not make any difference. However, I will argue in the following pages that there are theoretically and politically wide-ranging differences between the communities mentioned in this list. The crucially important difference is that the Amerindian communities mentioned were contemporaries of Hobbes and other classical writers, while the Amazon women, Saxon and other German families and the paternal communities of Ancient Greece were at best the predecessors of contemporary societies. Why is this distinction important? Because the claim is made that these societies represent an earlier stage of human development. Now, leaving aside whether this stage of development does actually have the meaning the classical writers attribute to it, it should nevertheless be clear that the claim that paternal communities in Ancient Greece represent an earlier stage in human development is at least in temporal terms correct. This, however, is not the case with the claim that the contemporary Amerindian societies represented an earlier stage in human development. In temporal terms they did not. The substantive philosophical point the classical writers want to make is, therefore, dependent on the example of the Amerindian societies. Not only theoretically but also politically is this an important distinction, at least from the point of view of constructing the international, for politically it does not matter much how we define and judge societies which do not exist any longer, while it matters crucially how we construct and define contemporary societies; legal rights and obligations, political practice and moral justifications of the relationship between European and Amerindian communities were based on the construction of these communities as representing a pre-civil state of development, as I will demonstrate in the following pages.

What then is the status of the writers of antiquity and the examples for communities in the state of nature taken from their writings? They are, I think, extremely important, but not as the trigger of these newly developing ideas for, after all, these writings had been known to the Europeans for quite some time without motivating such an abundance of writing on the state of nature. The discovery of the Amerindian communities and the need to integrate this phenomenon theoretically into the Christian *Weltanschauung*, as well as the need to define the political and moral framework within which to interact with these communities, was the trigger for this development among the Spanish authors from whom later European authors have taken over this modern concept of the state of nature which was supposedly represented by the Amerindian communities. The authors of antiquity, however, played a crucial role in this theoretical development on the one hand, because their authority was widely accepted and any supporting evidence one could find in their writings gave some weight and acceptance to the new ideas; on the other hand, the authors of antiquity as well as the Bible were widely reread and reinterpreted in the light of the experiences in the New World, so that Lafitau, for instance, could write on the *Customs of the American Indians Compared with the Customs of Primitive Times* (Lafitau, 1977; Haase and Meyer, 1994). Indeed, the simple fact that the Bible or Aristotle were read before and after the discovery of America does not tell us how these writings were read. It is impossible to establish exactly how much influence which source had quantitatively, although Ronald Meek, discussing this aspect very carefully, concludes that 'the fact that most of them [the classical writers developing the four-stage theory] drew so heavily upon the American studies and constantly emphasised their significance [...] seems to indicate that they may well have played a rather special role, perhaps going beyond that of a catalyst and approaching that of an independent primary source' (Meek, 1976: 3). My argument does in no way dispute the influence of Thucydides or other ancient writers on the classical authors or their use of examples taken from the ancient texts; it also does not depend on how important in quantitative terms the Amerindians were. Rather I will argue a qualitative point peculiar to the international: the example of ancient communities representing a state of nature does *not* set a precedent for the construction of the realm of international relations because, after all, one does not have to work out practical policies towards societies that do not exist any longer; the Amerindians, however, coexisted with the European nations at the time when the classical authors were writing and are, therefore, relevant for the construction of the international in a qualitatively different way.

And, finally, there is the last point at which my arguments might seem unfamiliar and counterintuitive. This is the conventional claim that the motivations of authors like Hobbes, Pufendorf, Rousseau and others are to be found in their experience of European and domestic developments like the English Civil War, the Thirty Years War and the Disintegration of the Holy Roman Empire and so on, and that these occasions provided the classical authors with the problems they attempted to solve in their theories (Boucher, 1998: 224f). What is implied in this claim is that the classical theories actually did not deliberately attempt to provide a theory of international relations as such, and that in so far as they did, they mainly dealt with the relationships among the European states rather than with the relationship between European and non-European peoples. It might therefore seem as if my interpretation of these authors exaggerates the relevance of their writings for international relations and overlooks the issues they attempted to deal with primarily. However, I am not arguing that the conception of international relations in general or the relationship between European and non-European peoples in particular were crucial issues in the writings of the classical political theorists. On the contrary, what I am arguing is that these theories concentrate on the redefinition and redesign of a universally valid *domestic* political organization which, however, crucially is built on the concept of the state of nature. This latter point has far-reaching implications for, on the one hand, it provides a basis for domestic political organization which itself was developed in the course of the international encounter with the Amerindians and, hence, entails certain assumptions about these non-European communities. Thus, having defined a universally valid form of domestic political organization in relation to a different and non-European form of political organization these theories *implicitly* define the proper relations between these different forms of political organization, that is international relations. Hence, I am not taking issue with the claim that these theories are motivated by particular European problems at the time; rather I am teasing out the role the international plays in the solutions offered as well as the implicit reconstruction of the international on the basis of these new domestic solutions.

Despite the fact that in Boucher's reading of the classical authors the importance of the concept of the state of nature is recognized and very intelligently dealt with, there is one link which Boucher is not able to make. And that is the link between this theoretical concept and the concrete peoples who are supposedly representing it. The conventional reading of classical political theory, I think, is to quite a great extent responsible for this missing link. First of all, if one examines the writings of a classical author within the limits of his explicit intention one has no basis from which to analyse the underlying assumptions, the building blocks for the realization of this intention. Or rather, even if one identifies the building blocks, like for example the concept of the state of nature, one does not necessarily look for their origins outside the defined scope of the work. There is a circular movement built into the procedure in that if Hobbes says he wants to solve the problem of civil wars in Europe, one looks in Europe for the theoretical and practical materials he uses in Europe. Secondly, because references to ancient European authors count as such weighty evidence and as accepted procedure, one does not easily question the function of this reference. For it might very well be the case that a classical thinker is quite extraordinarily motivated by political events in his time, but conforms to the accepted procedure in looking up and quoting corroborating evidence in classical authors, thus producing lists in which the Amerindians are, so to speak, hidden between more respectable classical sources. Thirdly, there is a tendency among political theorists and others to accept general pronouncements as truly abstract theoretical constructions, hence the *hypothetical* state of nature. However, if one accepts human beings as cultural beings, than one will have to look for the concrete contents of those theoretical pronouncements. For, as Geertz has argued, thoughts are not just happenings in the head, or, as Rousseau had pointed out, 'if you endeavour to trace in your mind the image of a tree in general, you never attain to your end. In spite of all you can do, you will have to see it as great or little, bare of leafy, light or dark, and were you capable of seeing nothing in it but what is common to all trees, it would no longer be like a tree at all' (Rousseau, 1993: 68). It would, then, be the task of a cultural analysis of classical political theory to search for the concrete contents of those abstract statements. Only then can we know their meaning.

And this is precisely what I intend to do in the next chapter. In order to avoid, as far as possible, all those pitfalls of traditional commentaries on classical political theory, I will not follow the conventional procedure. Since the object of the exercise is to 'excavate' the *unreflected* assumptions about non-European peoples in the construction of the international as well as their unintended consequences, I will systematically choose the Amerindians and their identification with the state of nature as an extra-European issue from which to analyse European political thought. This procedure has, just like the conventional one, its disadvantages. It will not allow me to provide a systematic and comprehensive analysis of the individual thinkers. But it will, hopefully, allow me to demonstrate something which is crucial as the basis for their thoughts and which they share. Hence, I will also not engage in elaborate attempts to analyse all the differences among them in detail and, thus, to distract from their commonalities with respect to the function of the extra-European world in their theories. But this does not mean that I intend to revise conventional interpretations of these authors, rather it means that I want to enrich our understanding of the differences among them by demonstrating certain commonalities which are extremely important for their *implicit* construction of the international, even in their domestic theories. I will also depart from the conventional history of ideas approach which demands a chronological order of the authors and an extensive discussion of who has taken what ideas from whom and how those have been reformulated in the process. Not only has Ronald Meek brilliantly and very carefully done this for the history of ideas leading up to the four-stage theory based on the state of nature (Meek, 1976), but I do not intend to concentrate on some intra-European theoretical development; I want to demonstrate the non-European element which has had such an important influence on European political theory, domestic and international.

6
The State of Nature as the Basis for Classical Political Thought

In this chapter, first of all, I will demonstrate that European classical authors have either widely identified the Amerindian peoples with human beings in the state of nature, or used the information about them in order to theoretically reconstruct an image of the state of nature. This was the common practice not only among political philosophers like Hobbes, Locke, Kant or Rousseau, but also among international lawyers like Pufendorf, Grotius and Vattel, as well as among political economists like Adam Smith and Ferguson, at the interface between literature and politics as in the case of Thomas More, Campanella, Montaigne and Francis Bacon, and by 'fathers' of sociology like Montesquieu. This indicates that the modern European social sciences, whose forerunners these authors are, are deeply pervaded with this concept of the state of nature and its identification with, or derivation from, the American Indians. It is interesting, too, that the concept of the state of nature did not play a crucial role in just one or two traditions which we know today as separate disciplines, but indeed equally in all of them. It was not the case, then, that only the early 'political economists' or the early 'political philosophers' or the early 'international lawyers' constructed their theories on the assumption of a state of nature. Indeed, it will be argued here that the concept of the state of nature was so fundamental for classical European thought on human society in general that it can be viewed as the common ground on which all modern European social sciences rest. Their subsequent division into different disciplines can be seen as the introduction of a plurality which – not only, of course, but also – clearly plays a role in covering up an orthodox basis common to all of them. It thus hides the cultural particularity of European social thought.

My choice of the above-mentioned authors is guided by the attempt to demonstrate precisely this, that the concept of the state of nature does indeed pervade European social thought on a very fundamental level and in all disciplines. This is also the reason why I have chosen to concentrate on authors that are fairly representative and often still cited today. There are, of course, other classical authors who have elaborated on the concept of the state of nature and its identification with the American Indian (see Meek, 1976; Echeverria, 1956; Bitterli, 1982). These authors might even, in some cases, have been much more important and well read at the time and they might have formulated some of the aspects even more clearly than the ones I concentrate on. But since the goal of this chapter is to demonstrate how our own thinking, inadvertently, rests on these assumptions I have chosen to concentrate on what we now consider an at least representative part of the 'canon of authoritative classical writers'. The reader will also find that this 'canon' does not contain Spanish authors any more. There are two reasons for this choice. Firstly, I want to show that the discovery of the American Indian was not only important for the formulation or reformulation of legal categories which might guide and justify practical policies. The discovery of the Amerindian peoples played an independent and crucial role for European thought on the nature, history and destiny of humankind, independently of any concrete material interests in America. From the publication of the Englishman Thomas More's *Utopia* in 1516, that is before the discovery of Mexico and long before the writings of Las Casas were printed and spread all over Europe, through Germans like Pufendorf and Kant who had no stake whatsoever in colonial adventures, the Englishman Locke and the Dutchman Grotius who were clearly inspired by concrete colonial politics, to Frenchmen like de Tocqueville who was more interested in *Democracy in America* (1835) than in colonial questions, we are confronted with European authors from all walks of life, so to speak, and with a huge variety of theoretical and practical interests in the subject matter. And this hints at the second reason for leaving Spanish authors out of this part of the study. For I want to show that in those more than three hundred years between 1516 and 1835, the discovery of America and the way in which it was taken up by European thinkers thoroughly changed European social thought. Whereas the early Spanish writings show the first signs of a break with a medieval European or Christian *Weltanschauung*, they are nevertheless very much aimed at rescuing those medieval beliefs. What becomes apparent in the subsequent theoretical development outside Spain is the increasing boldness with which the classical thinkers start to break with past conceptions and attempt to replace them with an alternative based on the concept of the state of nature.

And this, then, is the second aim of this chapter. It attempts to demonstrate that by the end of this period of classical European thought, that state of nature which was derived from the Amerindian experience had led to a radical redefinition of the nature, history and destiny of humankind. In other words, it had triggered a radical change in European culture. First of all, the discovery of the Amerindian peoples had, as we have seen already, fundamentally challenged the traditional religious belief in that state of nature identified with paradise and the subsequent fall from grace which underpinned the meaning and justification of societal institutions like government and property as punishment for original sin. It had challenged, too, the idea that all of humanity could eventually be traced back to Adam and Eve and that all peoples had been exposed to Christian teaching at one point or another. Thus, it challenged the authority of the Bible and other Christian texts and necessitated a new conception of the construction of valid knowledge. This new conception of how to arrive at valid knowledge was based on empirical study of the world rather than the traditional interpretation of the scriptures. The empirical study of humanity, however, included the representation of the newly discovered indigenous population in America as peoples in the state of nature, or close to it. This, in turn, necessitated the development of a new philosophy of history which would explain the different stages of human development and accommodate societies as radically different as the European and the Amerindian ones. Moreover, since Europeans traditionally built their societies on some conception of human nature, history and destiny, this new conception of what human nature was like and how it had developed historically over time allowed the European thinkers to criticize those aspects of the historical development of their own societies which did not seem to be in accordance with these new conceptions, and it therefore also led them to develop blueprints of various kinds for society properly based on human nature. These new societies, since they were thought to rest on a universal human nature, were also thought to be universally valid. And this assumption, in turn, led to a worldview based on a hierarchy of cultures. For, of course, once in possession of an ideal and universally valid concept of society, all real existing societies could be measured against it and placed on a linear scale in the order of their presumed approximation to the ideal. This chapter, then, will first deal with the new understanding of the construction of valid knowledge, followed by an exploration of the philosophies of history based on it, and an analysis of the conceptions of the ideal commonwealth. Finally, it will demonstrate the implications which all these developments in 'domestic' political and social thought had for the theoretical construction of the international.

The state of nature and the construction of social knowledge

Epistemologically, the unique significance of the Amerindians for European political thought lay in the possibility of deriving natural law – on which the Europeans traditionally based their societies – from a study of human nature itself. For, as Rousseau explained, any attempt to define true natural law by analysing European societies was prevented by the difficulty of distinguishing between the original and the artificially created in human nature (1993: 44). But the Amerindian societies were, in Montesquieu's view (1949: 294), almost entirely governed by nature and climate and, according to Tocqueville:

> exhibited none of those indistinct, incoherent notions of right and wrong, none of that deep corruption of manners, which is usually joined with ignorance and rudeness among nations who, after advancing to civilization, have relapsed into a state of barbarism. The Indian was indebted to no one but himself; his virtues, his vices, and his prejudices were his own work; he had grown up in the wild independence of his nature.
>
> (Tocqueville, 1994, I: 22)

And to Montaigne, these nations seemed to be 'so far barbarous, as having received but very little form and fashion from art and human invention, and consequently to be not much remote from their original simplicity. The laws of nature, however, govern them still, not as yet much vitiated with any mixture of ours' (Montaigne, 1990: 93). As a result of this same assumption, Locke concluded, that 'the Woods and Forests, where the irrational untaught Inhabitants keep right by following Nature, are fitter to give us Rules, than the Cities and Palaces, where those that call themselves Civil and Rational, go out of their way, by the Authority of Example' (1994: 182f). In the light of a real existing state of nature the interpretation of traditional scriptures could not claim any validity, as Locke in this case held against Filmer. And even though the Greeks had been closer to the state of nature than were the contemporary European societies, as Raynal and Diderot held (1969, I: 7),[1] 'the famous republics of antiquity never gave examples of more unshaken courage, more haughty spirit, or more intractable love of independence than were hidden in former times among the wild forests of the New World' (Tocqueville, 1994, I: 23). On the contrary, the Bible as well as the Greek writings were now themselves reinterpreted in the light of the discoveries (Pufendorf, 1927: xf).

If the Amerindians, as Pufendorf argued, were in the 'paradisical' state of nature while the Europeans found themselves in the world of sin, it now followed that the Bible, having derived from that early paradisical period, was valid for that period only. The natural law of the 'paradisical' period was, therefore, different from the natural law applicable in the degenerate historical state of humankind. Consequently, Pufendorf claimed that the science of natural law was totally different from moral theology in its method and demanded its independent status on the same grounds as medicine, mathematics and the natural sciences (1927: xi). The reading and interpretation of the scriptures dating from another period could not possibly produce any insight into contemporary natural law. The latter could only be analysed by research into the essence of human beings and into the common characteristics onto which their communal life is built and secured (Pufendorf, 1927: 17; Thomasius, 1950:[2] 1f, 8f, 39). By the time Adam Smith was writing, science was considered not just separate from religious beliefs but 'the great antidote to the poison of enthusiasm and superstition' (Smith, 1989: 347). Thus, the belief that the Amerindians represented a concrete historical state of nature became the basis for the development of social and political thought as a 'natural science'. When Ferguson, eventually, criticized his colleagues and predecessors for their approach, it was because it was not empirical enough for, 'in every other instance . . . the natural historian thinks himself obliged to collect facts, not to offer conjectures' as the European thinkers tended to do with respect to the state of nature (1995: 8). It was not any longer the interpretation of authoritative texts but the empirical study of human beings and their social life which would provide relevant insights into the nature of man and society. So, too, Hobbes had already refuted possible objections to his theory of absolute sovereignty by pointing out that 'if the Savage people of America should deny there were any grounds, or Principles of Reason' to build a house with new materials just because they had never seen them before, they would be wrong, for

> Time, and Industry, produce every day new knowledge. And as the art of well building is derived from Principles of Reason, observed by industrious men, that had long studied the nature of materials . . . so,

long time after men have begun to constitute Common-wealths, imperfect, and apt to relapse into disorder, there may Principles of Reason be found out, by industrious meditation, to make their constitution . . . everlasting.

(Hobbes, 1997: 232)

The art of building everlasting commonwealths, then, is likened to the art of building houses by applying reason to the nature of the materials. And if 'savages' cannot refute this procedure with respect to houses, then Europeans cannot refute this procedure – by arguing that these constitutions are traditionally unknown to them – with respect to the constitution of society. The Amerindian societies played a twofold role in this development of European thought, for, on the one hand, it was their discovery which had fundamentally discredited the traditional authoritative texts and, on the other hand, they were believed by all the European authors either to represent the state of nature, or to be much closer to it than the Europeans themselves or even the ancient Greeks and, thus, they became the preferred object of this empirical study.

The state of nature and the meaning of history

By introducing the state of nature as a universal condition from which humankind started its historical development the European authors introduced one linear timescale into the history of humanity. And, furthermore, the explanations which the European authors developed for the movement of humanity from one to the other stage of development justified and naturalized the particular European path of development – state-building, private property, money. For if, as Locke held, the Amerindians represented the 'Pattern of the first Ages in Asia and Europe', that is they represented the 'Infancy' of humankind, it followed that a single line had to be drawn between this infant state of humankind and the developed European (and Asian) societies (1994: 339f, 342). Accordingly, the Europeans developed a new philosophy of history based on linear historical time.[3] To be sure, they disagreed on the distinguishing features of the state of nature; in addition, some held the concept to be an ideal type (Hobbes, 1997: 89; Pufendorf, 1927: 90) while others made no such explicit distinction (Kant, 1996: 99, 103; Locke, 1994); and, finally, they disagreed on whether the Amerindian communities actually represented, approximated, or had long passed this condition (Rousseau, 1993: 65; 90f). Nevertheless, all these conceptions have two aspects in common. Firstly, it is the Amerindian 'material' to which they all apply their reason in order to derive an understanding of the state of nature. And secondly, in all cases the Amerindians are placed in a different historical time from the Europeans despite the fact that they were, of course, living at exactly the same time as the European observers. Thus, the discovery and particular placement of the Amerindian communities on that timescale provided the Europeans with a concrete second point beyond their own societies. They could now draw a line between those two fixed points – the European and the Amerindian – and extend this line into the future as well as into the past.

But drawing this historical line, of course, did not yet provide an explanation of how and why people have moved from one point on this line to the other, and without knowledge about the moving force behind this development the line could not be extended. The political thinkers developed various theories in order to explain this historical development, all of which justified and naturalized the particular European development – with the partial exception of Rousseau. Both Hobbes and Kant interpret the state of nature as a state of war in which human life is necessarily miserable and insecure. Reason and self-interest command that human beings leave this miserable state by setting up government and the rule of law over them – in short, by building states (Hobbes, 1997: 100f; Kant, 1996: 103). However, the same command does not apply to states because the latter are already the product of this reasonable freedom and, thus, cannot be placed under the obligation to give it up and consent to another law (Kant, 1996: 104; Hobbes, 1997: 149f). For Kant and Hobbes, thus, it is the very 'natural' freedom of the human being which is realized within states and therefore leads to a split between the natural law applicable within states as opposed to the one applicable between states. But since this theory locates the forces which drive people out of the state of nature into the historical development of state-building in the state of nature itself, it cannot explain why the Amerindians – theoretically endowed with as much reason as the Europeans – have not left the miserable state of nature, while the Europeans have.

Even though for Raynal, Diderot, Rousseau, Locke and others the state of nature is also characterized by the absence of law, government, private property, etc., it is not taken to constitute a state of war (Raynal, 1969, III: 404). These authors argue instead that if there is no private property there is no robbery, and where there is no robbery one does not need the law, the police and government in order to protect it (Raynal,

1969, II: 361; Locke, 1994: 302; Rousseau, 1993: 57f, 71ff, 90f; Smith, 1989: 309f). And the fairly peaceful existence of the Amerindian communities without a European-type government led to the assumption that they were held together by natural compassion (Rousseau, 1993: 73; Raynal, 1969, III: 404; Locke, 1994: 280f). Accordingly, Pufendorf comes to the conclusion that in the state of nature human beings can enter into a societal contract without having to build states and he believes that these societies were perfectly capable of satisfying the basic needs and desires of their members (1927: 103; also Locke, 1994: 299; Rousseau, 1993: 91f). In this account the state of nature does not provide an internal force which leads to any kind of development – it is a static condition reproducing itself.

However, comparing the Amerindians with the English, Locke comes to the conclusion that 'a King of a large and fruitful Territory there feeds, lodges, and is clad worse than a day Labourer in England' (1994: 296f; similarly Pufendorf, 1927: 17f; Raynal, 1969, III: 404ff; IV: 138ff; Rousseau, 1993: 195f). This scarcity plays a crucial role in the theories developed by these authors who generally assume that a widespread increase in population led to a scarcity of food and land which in turn led to fights over the scarce resources. These fights mark the end of a life according to natural law. State-building and the introduction of private property are depicted as the solutions to this dilemma: setting up a superior power over the community ensured peace between the members of the community, and the introduction of private property in land and its guarantee by the laws not only put an end to the fight over common resources but also provided the necessary conditions for intensive agriculture and, thus, raised production. Similarly the borders between states demarcate, so to speak, the private property in land of the different communities and thus – ideally – end the war between communities over common resources. Because state-building in this understanding leads to an increase in production and a decrease of wars, it ensures the possibility of living according to natural law under the conditions of an increase in the world's population and is therefore justified (Vattel, 1863: 97f; Pufendorf, 1927: 19).

Locke, coming to the same conclusion (1994: 302, 299), adds the invention of money as a condition for state-building because in his view the institution of private property is already present in the state of nature when the labour the Indian bestows on the common property 'makes the Deer, that Indian's who hath killed it' (1994: 287ff). But because 'nothing was made by God for Man to spoil or destroy' this perishable kind of private property cannot be accumulated and, therefore, does not lead to an increase in production (Locke, 1994: 290). It is in this sense that Locke came to the famous conclusion: 'Thus in the beginning all the World was America, and more so than that is now; for no such thing as Money was any where known. Find out something that hath the Use and Value of Money amongst his Neighbours, you shall see the same Man will begin presently to enlarge his Possessions' (1994: 301). The difference in material production between the 'savage nations of hunters and fishers' and 'civilized and thriving nations' clearly takes on a moral quality for, as Adam Smith put it:

> [The former] are so miserably poor that, from mere want, they are frequently reduced, or, at least, think themselves reduced, to the necessity sometimes of directly destroying, and sometimes of abandoning their infants, their old people, and those afflicted with lingering diseases, to perish with hunger, or to be devoured by wild beasts [while on the other hand in the latter] though a great number of people do not labour at all, many of whom consume the produce of ten times, frequently of a hundred times more labour than the greater part of those who work; yet the produce of the society is so great that...a workman, even of the lowest and poorest order...may enjoy a greater share of the necessaries and conveniences of life than it is possible for any savage to acquire.
>
> (Smith, 1989: 1)

In this account, the assumption of an increase in population plays a twofold role. It triggers the process of historical development, while at the same time justifying it. Even though in this case the driving forces of historical development are not located in the state of nature itself, these authors cannot explain the emergence of the crucial assumption of the increase in population. For if the state of nature indeed is static – just good enough for reproduction but not for growth of any kind – then where is the basis for the increase of population so crucial to the argument? Accordingly, Rousseau speculates about environmental circumstances as the trigger of development (1993: 92f, 95f, 98f), which in his view, by introducing private property, leads to the constitution of inequality in society (1993: 92). Nonetheless, although Rousseau's moral judgement is contrary to those of the others, all these theories share the introduction of one linear timescale into the history of humanity; all of them treat the Amerindian peoples – despite the fact that they share the same actual time with the European observers – as representatives of some earlier stage of human development; all of them justify the peculiar European institution of the state as in accordance with universal natural law; and, finally, all of them end up with two different kinds of natural law applicable to different stages of development.

The state of nature and the perfect commonwealth

The European authors, despite having thus justified state-building and private property as in accordance with natural law, did not overlook the shortcomings of their own societies. Having finally discovered or redis-covered the true natural law they set out to conceive an ideal and universally valid society based on human nature. In contrast to earlier conceptions this was a secular society which could be realized by human effort in time. 'The Indians', said Tocqueville, 'although they are ignor-ant and poor, are equal and free' (1994, I: 23). And if equality and freedom were natural qualities of man, then these had to be realized in any society which claimed to be organized according to natural law. It was the example of the Amerindian peoples which left Locke in no doubt whatsoever, that 'Men are naturally free, and the Examples of History shewing, that the Governments of the World . . . had their begin-ning laid on that foundation, and were made by the Consent of the People' which was the 'Right', the 'Opinion' and the 'Practice of Man-kind, about the first erecting of Governments' (1994: 336). In Locke's account the development of despotic or absolute power – a deviation from natural law – can only be set right if the legislature is placed in 'collective Bodies of Men, call them Senate, Parliament, or what you please' (1994: 329f.). Thus, the Amerindian communities and their particular form of government – as perceived by Locke – provide him with a concrete value which has been lost in the course of historical development.

> And if the speculative would find that habitual state of war which they are sometimes pleased to honour with the name of *the state of nature*, they will find it in the contest that subsists between the despotical prince and his subjects, not in the first approaches of a rude and simple tribe to the condition and the domestic arrange-ments of nations.
>
> (Ferguson, 1995: 73)

On this basis the European reformers attacked absolutism and despotic government which they now held to violate freedom as a natural right of human beings.

The natural right of freedom was, of course, based on the assumption of a natural equality of human beings which was also conspicuously absent from European societies. Though in the state of nature human beings were born in equality, Montesquieu argued, in society they lost this equality and only regained it through the laws (1949: 111; similarly Locke, 1994: 271; Raynal, 1969, III: 404; Pufendorf, 1927: ch. 7, §1; Rousseau, 1993: 80). Thus, equality before the law became one of the crucial goals of the reformers.

> If the men of our time should be convinced, by attentive observation and sincere reflection, that the gradual and progressive development of social equality is at once the past and the future of their history, this discovery alone would confer upon the change the sacred character of a divine decree.
>
> (Tocqueville, 1994, I: 7)

The major elements of the new philosophy of history are apparent in this statement by de Tocqueville, for if equality is the universal past of humankind then it also has to be the universal future of humankind – the ontological universality has to be realized. The means by which one arrives at this knowledge are 'attentive observation' and 'sincere reflection' – and in no way either the interpretation of the scriptures or the 'authority of historical examples' because they only reflect historically outdated values on the one hand or particular historical developments which had deviated from the universally valid natural law on the other. And, finally, the politics leading to the realization of social equality is sanctified through the 'discovery' of its historical roots – the goal is ethical and therefore justifies the means.

But if the European authors interpret the Amerindian communities as representing certain natural law values which have to be taken up and realized in a universally valid society this does not mean that they want to return to a state of nature. Having established that states are in accordance with natural law at this particular stage in historical development they distinguish between natural and civil liberty. The former, being 'common to man with beasts and other creatures', is 'inconsistent with authority' and in time 'makes men grow more evil and...worse than brute beasts', while the latter can only be found in the 'moral law and the politic covenants and constitutions among men themselves' and 'it is a liberty to that only which is good, just, and honest' (Tocqueville 1994, I: 42). Similarly, since natural equality was based on common property but the laws, those 'politic covenants and constitutions', are based on private property, civil equality is essentially different from the original natural one (Locke, 1994: 350f; Raynal, 1969, III: 411ff; Montesquieu, 1949: 56, 111). Therefore, Raynal and Diderot argue, the ideal society has to be built on private property the basis of which must be the equal distribution of land; and Tocqueville identifies the abundance of land in the US as the very basis of democracy because the social equality of the Americans depends on it (Tocqueville, 1994, I: 290f; Raynal, 1969, VI: 113; Rousseau, 1993: 240). Unlike in America, in Europe the attempt to realize this ideal society proved to be much more difficult and disruptive since it continuously encountered traditional forces, as, for example, the French Revolution demonstrated (Tocqueville, 1994, I: 291f). However, just as the European authors split the supposedly universal natural law in the course of the development of their new philosophy of history, in practice the universal values of equality and freedom only applied to those members of society who were reasonable enough to comprehend them. Women, children, madmen and slaves (on the basis of their race) were excluded because nature had not (yet) furnished them with enough reason, and civil slaves were excluded because they could not own property and, hence, could not be expected to consent to and uphold laws based on property (Locke, 1994: 304f, 307f, 332f, 174; Pufendorf, 1927: 97; Tocqueville, 1994, I: 379f; II: 211f; Montesquieu, 1949: 252).

The discovery of the Amerindian societies was crucial for this new concept of a universally valid society based on natural law because despite the fact that in their interpretation of the Amerindian societies the Europeans were strongly led by their own cultural values – the idea that the state of nature is based on common property is, for example, an integral part of traditional Christian belief – no other contemporary society could have substantiated this belief. Equality and freedom were clearly not distinguishing features of Chinese, Muslim or Indian societies. And the fact that the historical scriptures, including the Bible, described societies characterized by common property, a nomadic lifestyle and government by some kind of political consensus did not prove anything else but that all societies possibly had their beginning there but all of them also seemed to have moved out of this developmental stage. The fact that the Amerindians lived like that today challenged the belief that the development of social inequality and despotic government was natural and inevitable and led the Europeans to reinterpret the ancient writers in the light of this new discovery (Lafitau, 1977). And, finally, the gap between the naked and savage Indians without tools or religious and political institutions, roaming the woods, and the Europeans with their sophisticated dress code, their ordered political and religious institutions, and their advanced material way of life was so big that there seemed to be no limit to human progress (Lestringant, 1994: 174). In the course of this theoretical development, stretching over three centuries, the Golden Age which previously had been located in the past, in antiquity, gradually came to be placed in the future, the Christian *telos* of salvation replaced by a secular *telos* of human development (Cro, 1994: 388f; Pagden, 1993: 93, 111, 115).

That the discovery of America and the Amerindian societies triggered the production of blueprints for the perfect commonwealth is, of course, also apparent in the utopian literature, in the societies depicted by Thomas More's *Utopia*, Tommaso Campanella's *City of the Sun* and even in Francis Bacon's *New Atlantis*. New Atlantis is governed by a caste of high priests belonging to the House of Salomon. But these priests are scientists and their goal is 'the knowledge of Causes, and secret motions of things; and the enlarging of the bounds of Human Empire, to the effecting of all things possible' (Bacon, 1996: 480). So, too, the Utopians 'have learned every single useful art of the Roman civilisation...and made themselves masters of all our useful inventions', while the City of the Sun is governed by priests according to the best of all the arts and sciences which have ever been practised and invented by any people in the world (More, 1993: 41; Campanella, 1981: 33–7, 43–5, 95–7). Thus, although religion is very much present, it is through the worldly pursuit of the sciences that it validates itself in the utopian societies. But, for the purposes of this study, it is even more interesting, how these utopian societies come to gain their knowledge of the arts and sciences. While the Utopians have learned from a chance encounter with Romans and Egyptians in the past, the people of the City of the Sun regularly send out ambassadors all over the world to learn from other societies; and the House of Salomon sends out twelve ships to sail to other countries under the name of other nations '(for our own we conceal), who bring us the books, and abstracts, and patterns of experiments of all other parts. These we call Merchants of Light' (Bacon, 1996: 486; More, 1993: 41; Campanella, 1981: 37). Knowledge, the sciences, then, are gained through visiting other nations, openly or under cover, and the best which is found in those other cultures is introduced in the utopian societies. The City of the Sun as well as Utopia is based on the principle of common property and the election of government officials (More, 1993: 37, 48f; Campanella, 1981: 39, 43–5). Thus, not only do we find the crucial elements of Amerindian societies, as perceived by the

European thinkers – common property and political liberty – constitutive of the utopian societies, but they clearly acknowledge the inspiration drawn from foreign nations.

Yet, irrespective of whether one is inclined to embrace or reject the utopian societies depicted here, for the scholar of International Relations what is most interesting are their relations with foreign nations. Convinced of having achieved the highest possible order in comparison with other societies, they protect themselves from outsiders. King Utopus, who originally conquered the country and

> brought its rude, uncouth inhabitants to such a high level of culture and humanity that they now excel in that regard almost every other people, also changed its geography. After subduing the natives... he promptly cut a channel... where their land joined the continent, and thus caused the sea to flow around the country.
>
> (More 1993: 43)

This is, indeed, a very meaningful act, for the Utopians do not use the water around them only to more easily defend themselves but, more importantly, they try to keep strangers away, they conduct their trade abroad rather than at home, they jealously guard the intercourse between the Utopian population and that of other nations; this they do in order to prevent the backward social ideas and practices of other peoples from spreading and infecting their own population, in addition to the chance of gathering information about their neighbours (More, 1993: 79f). This, however, does not mean that they do not have an active foreign policy which consists of sending magistrates to rule neighbouring countries that they have liberated from tyranny; they also engage in wars helping their friends and allies and liberating oppressed people from tyrants and servitude 'in the name of humanity'; if they enter into war they first try to assassinate the tyrant of the other party, then tend to use a savage tribe as mercenaries in order to save their own soldiers and never worry about how many of the former get killed 'for they think they would deserve well of all mankind if they could exterminate from the face of the earth that entire vicious and disgusting race'; but if and when the Utopians go to war they themselves are as cruel and vicious as possible in order to deter others (1993: 85–92). Furthermore, whenever the population of Utopia rises beyond a certain point the excess is sent out to the mainland to build colonies; if the natives accept the laws of the Utopians, the two nations blend, but those who refuse to live under their laws the Utopians drive out of the land they claim for themselves; and on those who resist them, they declare war. The Utopians say it's perfectly justifiable to make war on people who leave their land idle and waste yet forbid the use and possession of it to others who, by the law of nature, ought to be supported from it.

(More, 1993: 56)

Apart from the fact that More here discusses the European justifications for colonization, it is interesting that, despite the fact that this perfect commonwealth is built on 'the kinship of nature' among men, the Utopians feel that they have to keep others out of their commonwealth while at the same time conducting quite a 'missionizing' foreign policy with other nations who are ranked according to their approximation and reciprocation of Utopian ideals and practices.

Indeed, we find a very similar set up in New Atlantis. Whereas, on the one hand, the inhabitants of New Atlantis keep their own island, their own existence, hidden from other nations, on the other they send out their messengers – today we might call this industrial espionage – to bring back books and inventions from other nations. However, at the end of the fragment, the traveller who has learned about the wonderful institutions of New Atlantis is sent back into the known world, given 'leave to publish it for the good of other nations' (Bacon, 1996: 488). Unlike the other two societies, the City of the Sun is indeed open to travellers and displays its institutions proudly. Nevertheless, here too we find, apart from defensive wars, wars for the liberation of other oppressed nations in which 'the warrior who slays the tyrant receives the prize of spoils' (Campanella, 1981: 75). Defeated enemies 'immediately change over to the system of communal ownership of all goods... and proceed to model their institutions after those' of the City of the Sun (1981: 77). The missionizing character of this kind of foreign policy does not actually rest on particular institutions in those societies, but on the conviction that they are not just practically but also morally the best possible social order for all human societies; while foreign ideas are taken up by the utopian societies and realized in a perfect domestic order, their foreign policy subsequently spreads those ideas to other peoples. And this is exactly, as we shall see in the next section, the implication of the domestic theories of the classical thinkers outlined above for the international sphere.

The state of nature and the hierarchy of cultures

The philosophy of history which the Europeans had developed, together with their new concept of a legitimate political community based on natural law, inevitably led to a *Weltanschauung* based on a hierarchy of cultures. Though natural law by definition was supposed to be universal we have already seen that the Europeans had ended up with two different kinds of natural law – one applying to the original state of nature, the other to the developed historical stage of mankind. And not only that, but in the developed historical stage of mankind it was the state with its domestic laws which ensured and embodied the developed natural law while between the states the rules of the original natural law still more or less applied (Locke, 1994: 357; Hobbes, 1997: 90; Kant, 1996: 102; Rousseau, 1993: 99f). Over time this analogy of the state of nature between individuals and the state of nature between states was increasingly questioned (Vattel, 1863: xiiif).

Vattel, therefore, distinguished between necessary and voluntary international law – necessary international law being the original natural law and voluntary international law being the positive law which civilized states have agreed upon (1863: 381ff; Grotius, 1925: 393f, 42ff). On this basis the rights and responsibilities of voluntary international law were not extended to 'wild' and 'barbaric' peoples. The Amerindians, because they had not yet built states and introduced private property, did not conform to the law of nature which applied in this historical phase. Locke uses these cultural distinctions, for example, when he argues that in the state of nature land which is common can be appropriated and enclosed by anyone, while 'Land that is common in England, or any other Country, where there is Plenty of People under Government, who have Money and Commerce' cannot be enclosed or appropriated by outsiders because, 'though it be Common in respect of some Men, it is not so to all Mankind; but is the joint property of this Country' (Locke, 1994: 292). Vattel even argues that every political community is free to choose its internal constitution as it likes and, thus, can introduce common property as described in Campanella's *City of the Sun*. Outsiders have to respect the land which is held in common property as the private property of that political community (1863: 163f). But crucially this general universal rule does not apply to other cultures on a different level of historical development. In his discussion of the expropriation of the Amerindian communities of North America, Vattel applies the original natural law which obliges everyone to support the species in general. Since the European states are overpopulated, he argues, nomadic peoples like the Amerindians of North America or the Bedouins of the Arabian desert can be forced to live on a smaller piece of land where they have to practise intensive agriculture and, thereby, make the rest of their land available for the needy European populations. Though the Spanish conquest of Mexico and Peru is considered illegal because those were 'well ordered states' and the Spanish brutalities are generally criticized vehemently by the other European authors, they all justify the expropriation of the nomadic Amerindians on these grounds (Vattel, 1863: 35f, 155, 163f, 170f; Hobbes, 1997: 239; Locke, 1994: 291f).

Similarly with respect to the laws of war Vattel holds that barbaric peoples have to be considered enemies of mankind and every state has a right to fight wars against them, even if it has not been harmed by them at all (1863: 304f). Indeed, not only the *jus ad bellum* but also the *jus in bello* differs significantly. Thus, if an army in the course of war has to cross the territory of another civilized state it has to surrender its arms while the latter would not only be unnecessary but even irresponsible if it crossed the territory of a wild people; similarly, one may not destroy the country of a civilized enemy in war but the destruction of the country of a barbaric nation is not only allowed but even a positive goal because it provides an opportunity to punish the barbarians; and while one has to distinguish between combatants and non-combatants and officers and soldiers in war with a civilized nation, one may catch and punish any member of a barbaric nation who are all guilty by definition – these strict measures are supposed to force them to acknowledge the humanitarian law (Vattel, 1863: 342f, 367f, 348).

However, not only in international law but also in political theory genocidal practices were justified on the basis of this new philosophy of history. De Tocqueville, for example, recognizes the treatment of the Amerindian peoples (and the slaves) in North America in its brutal reality, when he says, 'if we reason from what passes in the world, we should almost say that the European is to other races of mankind what man himself is to the lower animals: he makes them subservient to his use, and when he cannot subdue he destroys them' (1994, I: 332). But while, according to de Tocqueville, the Spaniards, despite all their atrocities, never quite managed to deprive the Amerindians of their rights or to 'exterminate the Indian race', the 'Americans of the United States have accomplished this twofold purpose with singular felicity, tranquilly, legally, philanthropically, without shedding blood, and without violating a single great principle of morality in the eyes of the world. It is impossible to destroy men with more respect for the laws of humanity'

(1994, I: 354f). Although Tocqueville analyses this process and explicitly names the actors and the deliberate policies by which they achieve their ends – and he clearly deplores the fate of the Amerindians – it is described by him as tragic but inevitable (1994, I: 350f). And the reason for this inevitability is precisely that philosophy of history and the laws, domestic and international, that go with it. Because despite the fact that North America was inhabited by countless Indian tribes when the Europeans got there

> it may justly be said ... to have formed one great desert. The Indians occupied without possessing it. It is by agricultural labour that man appropriates the soil, and the early inhabitants of North America lived by the produce of the chase. ... They seem to have been placed by Providence amid the riches of the New World only to enjoy them for a season; they were there merely to wait till others came. Those coasts so admirably adapted for commerce and industry; those wide and deep rivers; that inexhaustible valley of the Mississippi; the whole continent, in short, seemed prepared to be the abode of a great nation yet unborn. In that land the great experiment of the attempt to construct society upon a new basis was to be made by civilized man; and it was there, for the first time, that theories hitherto unknown, or deemed impracticable, were to exhibit a spectacle for which the world had not been prepared by the history of the past.
>
> (Tocqueville, 1994, I: 25).

The universal validity of what Tocqueville called the 'triumphal march of civilization across the desert' is not at all put into question by the necessary extinction of the Amerindian communities because in the last analysis it is their own backwardness which does not allow them to assimilate fast enough in order to fit into the new society. Therefore, 'they perish if they continue to wander from waste to waste, and if they attempt to settle they still must perish' (1994, I: 354).

But not only did the peoples who were still thought to be in or very close to the state of nature have to occupy their appropriate place on that linear timescale of history, once that scale existed all cultures had to be located on it. Since it was inconceivable that development could take place in a way different from the European one, the Enlightenment authors concluded that the Spanish reports on the cultural achievements of the Mexicans – who had actually set up a 'well ordered state' and were not taken to be in the state of nature – must simply be false, or 'greatly exaggerated', as Smith put it (Smith, 1989: 191). Mexican culture had to be young, had in fact barely left the state of nature, and was for this reason characterized by the most incredible despotism and superstition, i.e. violation of natural law (Raynal, 1969, II: 397ff). Mexico, then, ranked clearly underneath China, Japan and India but above the hunting stage (Smith, 1989: 191, 276). The tremendous age of Indian culture, on the other hand, could not be doubted. Hence, Indian culture was – for reasons of climate and the caste system – considered stagnant, its laws, manners, lifestyle, clothes were supposed to be the same today as they were a thousand years ago, and the same applied to China, according to Smith (Montesquieu, 1949: 225, 269; Raynal, 1969, I: 38ff; Smith, 1989: 40). The Indians, although they were an old culture, were like children and so were the Mexicans as a new culture. Accordingly, argue Raynal and Diderot, the wild peoples 'want' to be guided by gentleness and held back by force. Since they are incapable of governing themselves their government has to be enlightened and they have to be guided by violence till they reach the age of insight. Therefore barbaric peoples live quite 'naturally' under despotism until the progress of society has taught them to be guided by their own interest (Raynal, 1969, VI: 110; Montesquieu, 1949: 225).

The universal law based on human nature and considered to be in the interest of all of humankind, then, led ironically to the introduction of different kinds of law applying to different cultures, depending on their ranking on this universal evolutionary scale. It is interesting to note that, confronted with cultural differences, the Europeans by this time had not progressed any further than the Spaniards had three hundred years earlier. For, either the cultural differences were identified with distinct political communities, in which case a radical distinction is made between domestic and international law, defining the international realm out of the reach of the level of morality in the domestic realm – this position is close to Vitoria's – or the cultural differences were interpreted as distinctions within humanity as a whole, in which case all those peoples who did not live up to the highest stage of development could be ruled by the more enlightened ones, that is simply incorporated on a lower level into the 'domestic' realm. This would have been Sepúlveda's position. But before we return to the implications of these theoretical developments for the discipline of International Relations, I will demonstrate in the next chapter that the influence of the discovery of the Amerindians pertained not only to domestic political and social theory but also to domestic practice in Europe and America.

7
The Politics of the State of Nature in the American and French Revolutions

In the previous chapter I have argued that the concept of the state of nature played an important role not just for the construction of the international but also for the redefinition of the domestic political community in European thought. But, as I will suggest in this chapter, this was not just a theoretical development. The concept of the state of nature came to play an important role in the practical constitution of modern Western states as I will show with respect to the Constitution of the United States of America as well as the French Revolution.

That this should have been the case in North America is not too surprising for, after all, the white Americans were in close interaction with the Amerindian population from the moment they set foot on the American continent. They were, for instance, dependent on Amerindian food production. And this was not just the case in the very early years of English settlements: even during the revolution, Franklin argued that the 'Americans' could afford to boycott English products because they could replace them with and live off 'Indian corn' (Venables, 1992: 105). Likewise, the English in America had been dependent on the fur trade with the Amerindians and on their military support right up to the revolution; and, here again, apart from the fact that the Amerindians were fighting in the revolutionary wars on both sides, Franklin suggested that the 'Americans' defend themselves against the English by adopting Amerindian fighting techniques (McFarlane, 1994: 80f; Venables, 1992: 105). But, most importantly, the Amerindians were 'occupying' the land on which the white Americans wanted to establish their own society. And it was this conflict over the land which played a role in bringing about the revolution in the first place and had a lasting impact on the Constitution of the United States of America.

It needs to be pointed out, first of all, that the English discourse on the conquest and colonization of America with respect to the Amerindians, right from the start, was no different from the Spanish one. That is, not only did the English very early on translate Spanish reports on the New World, but they considered their own role and the nature of the Amerindians in a very similar way to the Spaniards. Despite their rivalry with Catholic Spain, they even defended the Spaniards against the critique that the missionary enterprises in the New World were only a justifying veil behind which the real goal of the Spaniards, gold, was hidden. For in the eyes of the protestant English there was no question whatsoever that 'Christianity and profit could well complement each other' (Williams, 1992: 130; McFarlane, 1994: 25f). Not only were the Amerindians seen as people in the state of nature in the sense of the absence of culture, as 'a smooth and bare table unpainted . . . upon the which you may at the first paint or write what you list, as you cannot upon tables already painted', as Richard Eden pronounced, but that which the English wanted to 'paint and write on these bare tables' was the same that Spaniards had tried to write on their 'bare tables', namely Christianity and civility (cf. Williams, 1992: 130f). Not only did the English believe that the Amerindians, being 'bare tables', would take on Christianity easily and with gratitude, but they also compared them favourably with the 'Jews and Turks', as 'tables' which had already been inscribed, just like the Spaniards had done (Williams, 1992: 130f, 171, 182). And just like the Spaniards, the English argued that the Amerindians, violating natural laws, did not have any rights in their land; the English could lead just wars against them (1992: 194, 196).

To be sure, there were differences between the English and the Spanish practice of colonization. But, to begin with, the English were motivated by the same goals as were the Spaniards, together with others resulting from their competition with Spain. These were: to find the same riches the Spaniards had found and bolstered their power in Europe with; to import the goods which used to come from the Mediterranean instead from America; to find an alternative route to Asia; to establish a basis in America from which to attack Spanish ships; to 'export' or 'replant' the poor from overpopulated England to America and establish new markets for English products; to 'replant' English Catholics to America; and to Christianize the native population (McFarlane, 1994: 25f). In so far as there were differences between the Spanish and the English, these were due to the different conditions they found and not to a different normative conception of, and approach to, the indigenous population. First of all, the English did not find gold and silver as the Spaniards had done and, secondly, they did not find anything resembling the Aztec and Inca Empires which would allow them to set themselves up over an already centralized and highly populated area (1994: 193f). While the settlers in Virginia were, like the Spaniards, clearly more interested in making a profit – they did not grow foodstuffs but tobacco and the Virginia Company, in the beginning, only sent men to America – the Puritans in the North were more interested in establishing their own Christian communities than to use, as the Spaniards had done, the Amerindian 'human material' for such a purpose (1994: 41, 45, 47).

Notwithstanding these differences, the Amerindians played quite a crucial role in the revolution, for the conduct of the settlers and their encroachment upon Amerindian land had, by the middle of the seventeenth century, led to attacks and regular wars by the Amerindians against the settlers. While the settlers wanted to respond with violent counter-attacks, the Crown attempted to get the situation under control by guaranteeing the land of the Amerindians beyond a certain line. This was unacceptable for the settlers who were, in addition, unwilling to pay for the garrisons which would protect them against Amerindian attacks and the Amerindians against the settler's attacks (1994: 198f, 200f, 253f). Thus, the discourse on the legal rights of the Amerindians in land played a crucial role in the years before the American Revolution.

The initial justification for British colonization in America was very much in line with that of the Spaniards. The Charter of the Virginia Company stated unmistakably that the English task in America 'by the Providence of Almighty God' consisted in 'propagating of Christian Religion to such People, as yet live in Darkness and miserable Ignorance of the true Knowledge and Worship of God, and may in time bring the Infidels and Savages, living in those Parts, to human Civility, and to a settled and quiet Government' (cf. Williams, 1992: 201). The Amerindians were considered only to 'occupy' the land 'as wild beasts in the forests' without any kind of law, government or property, so that 'if the whole land should be taken from them, there is not a man that can complain of any particular wrong done unto him' (cf. Williams, 1992: 211). Hence, because of the lack of private property, individuals could not complain, and because of the lack of law and government, they could not be recognized as independent political communities with community rights.

This consensus, however, broke down in the course of the development of English settlements in America because there were, essentially, three different parties with three different kinds of interests involved. Firstly, there was the British Crown which denied, for cultural reasons, the rights of the Amerindians and derived its own rights from 'discovery' and conquest which established a royal prerogative (Williams, 1992: 221, 229). The settlers, however, desirous of the land the Amerindians occupied, denied that these rights of the Crown were established law. But they were split, too, because it was in the interest of the landless states, that is states without a royal charter, to be able to buy land directly from the Amerindians. This, of course, could not be done in the face of a royal prerogative and a denial that the Amerindians owned their land legally in the first place. The landed states, those who had a royal charter like Virginia, for instance, on the other hand would gain more if individual speculators were not allowed to buy land directly from the Amerindians without any control of the state (1992: 229f).

This conflict of interests would later have far-reaching repercussions for the Constitution of the United States of America. For the speculators from the landless states lobbied strongly for Congress to recognize that the Amerindians legally owned their land and, therefore, had the right to sell it without interference. Grotius and Pufendorf were cited in support of this position (Williams, 1992: 230, 309). The landed states, however, lobbied for the recognition that the Amerindians as 'infidels, heathens, and savages' did not have the prerogative rights over the land a European derived government had and, therefore, the latter should have control over the frontier lands (1992: 230). With this argument, however, they found themselves in a difficult situation, for on the one hand they traced their own rights to independence from Britain back to a state of nature in general and that of the freedom-loving Saxons in particular and denied the rights of the British Crown derived from the Norman Conquest. Jefferson argued that under Saxon natural law conditions property was held absolutely by individuals. The Normans, he held, had superimposed their own feudal law of conquest to which the Saxons, indeed, never really had surrendered (1992: 268f). But this argument against the rights of the British Crown was simultaneously an argument against the rights of the landed states in America, whose royal charter was, of course, based on exactly that alien and feudal right of conquest. The landed states, therefore, made the argument that their governments did, indeed, have a prerogative which was, however, not derived from conquest but from the natural liberty of man which the American form of government, that is democracy, embodied and guaranteed (1992: 287). A compromise was eventually achieved between the interests of the landed and those of the landless states, in which the landed states had to cede their rights into the western lands to the Federal Government. And the Federal Government did, indeed, have the right to 'extinguish Indian occupancy claims by purchase or conquest' (1992: 231). Hence, the independence of America from Britain was based on an argument derived from the state of nature – as we shall see shortly – namely that human beings have a natural right to liberty, while the relationship between the Amerindians and the Federal Goverment was based on the feudal rights of conquest.

The one classical author who played a seminal role in this American discourse was, of course, John Locke. For not only did he derive the right of liberty from the state of nature, but also the right of property. His discussion of the liberty right could be used by the Americans against British colonial rule, and his definition of property rights could be asserted against the Amerindians who supposedly did not practice agriculture and, therefore, had to cede this right to the more advanced nation who did (Tonsor, 1990: 121f; Williams, 1992: 246ff). That his position fitted the needs of the Americans so neatly does, of course, not come as much of a surprise for, after all, Locke had worked for the Carolina Company, assisted in drawing up the colony's first constitution, and had also worked for the Board of Trade (McFarlane, 1994: 110f). That the 'Founding Fathers' of the United States of America thus quoted not only Locke and Montesquieu but also their practical experiences with the Amerindians frequently in their discussions was not too surprising. The first two of the three crucial values of the American Constitution – life, liberty and property – were frequently identified with the native Americans from whose state of nature they were derived (cf. Venables, 1992: 75f, 77, 84).

The Articles of Confederation and the American Revolution secured life and liberty better than property. Hence, the Constitution was supposed to redress that balance. And, interestingly enough, in this context we also find another idea expressed earlier by Enlightenment writers. The establishment of a central Federal Government was, as we have seen, on the one hand necessary to resolve the conflict between the landed and the landless states. This central government, however, seemed to contradict the political arguments of the Enlightenment authors as well as of the Americans themselves who had argued against British rule that their own governments embodied the natural right of liberty. John Adams and Madison defended the central government with the argument that, although the Americans based their rights to liberty in a state of nature likened to the Germanic tribes, this time, history also demonstrated that these decentralized political communities were vulnerable to the greater power of more centralized forms of government. Hence, first the Roman and subsequently the Norman conquest of Britain. If, then, Americans wanted to be able to defend themselves and their liberties against such attacks, they would have to set up a central government (Venables, 1992: 119f). In their conflict with Britain, the white Americans, then, repeatedly referred to and based their rights on various peoples in the state of nature – Amerindians, Germanic tribes, Saxons – neatly symbolized by the Boston Tea Party in which the rebels who threw the tea overboard had dressed up as Mohawks (1992: 74).

Let us have a look, then, at a central figure bringing together the American and the French Revolutions. Thomas Paine not only conversed with Franklin, Jefferson and Washington among others, he also held office in America. He served as a secretary to the Foreign Affairs Committee of the Continental Congress and later became clerk of the Pennsylvania Assembly. Paine wrote passionately for American independence and does, indeed, reproduce all the important concepts the Enlightenment writers used, including the link to the Amerindians. First of all, Paine argued exactly like other Enlightenment writers with respect to the proper method of establishing knowledge not just about external nature, but also about human societies.

> Every art and science, however imperfectly known at first, has been studied, improved, and brought to what we call perfection, by the progressive labours of succeeding generations; but the science of government has stood still. No improvement has been made in the principle, and scarcely any in the practice, till the American revolution began. In all the countries of Europe (except in France) the same forms and systems that were erected in the remote ages of ignorance, still continue, and their antiquity is put in the place of principle; it is forbidden to investigate their origin, or by what right they exist. If it be asked, how has this happened? the answer is easy; they are established on a principle that is false, and they employ their power to prevent detection.
>
> (Paine, 1995: 387)

Hence, Paine established that the 'science of government' has made no progress because men were prevented from investigating its principles. But how, then, could one establish the right principles? Well, 'to understand what the state of society ought to be, it is necessary to have some idea of the natural and primitive state of man; such as it is at this

day among the Indians of North America' (1995: 416). And 'it is only by
tracing things to their origins that we can gain rightful ideas of them'
(1995: 418). Thomas Paine followed his own advice and applied this
method in particular to the question of the origins and development of
government, of inequality and of property. In the state of nature
government did not exist. 'For as nature knows them [Kings] *not*, they
know *not her*, and although they are beings of our *own* creating,
they know not *us*, and are become the gods of their creators' (Paine,
1995: 47). For Paine there is no question whatsoever that 'He, who hunts
the woods for prey, the naked and untutored Indian, is less a Savage
than the King of Britain' (Paine, 1995: 47). And Paine argued that it is
man in the state of nature from whom the right principles of government have to be derived. For 'if any generation of men ever possessed
the right of dictating the mode by which the world should be governed
for ever, it was the first generation that existed' (Paine, 1995: 117). The
first generation of men, he was convinced, did not know governments
(1995: 121, 11). Governments were developed 'when a set of artful men
pretended, through the medium of oracles, to hold intercourse with the
Deity, as familiarly as they now march up the backstairs in European
courts, the world was completely under the government of superstition'
(1995: 121). The first introduction of government, then, can be put
down to superstition and ignorance, but 'after these a race of conquerors
arose, whose government, like that of William the Conqueror, was
founded in power, and the sword assumed the name of the scepter'
(1995: 121).

Over and against government, Paine held up society for which man
was truly made by nature.

> As Nature created him [man] for social life, she fitted him for the
> station she intended. In all cases she made his natural wants greater
> than his individual powers. No one man is capable, without the aid
> of society, of supplying his own wants; and those wants, acting
> upon every individual, impel the whole of them into society, as
> naturally as gravitation acts to the center [so that] in short, man is
> so naturally a creature of society, that it is almost impossible to put
> him out of it.
>
> (Paine, 1995: 214f)

Society, thus, is prior to government, and 'all the great laws of society
are laws of nature' in the sense that they are rooted in the nature of
man (Paine, 1995: 216). Society could function perfectly without

government and was based on the nature of man, was intended by nature, whereas government was based on the sword (1995: 220).

On the basis of these arguments, Paine derived the *Rights of Man* from nature, from the first man. 'Though I mean not to touch upon any sectarian principle of religion, yet it may be worth observing, that the genealogy of Christ is traced to Adam. Why then not trace the rights of man to the creation of man?' (1995: 117). And if we take a look at this first generation what we find is that

> every history of the creation, and every traditionary account, whether from the lettered or unlettered world, however they may vary in their opinion or belief of certain particulars, all agree in establishing one point... that all men are born equal, and with equal natural right... and consequently, every child born into the world must be considered as deriving its existence from God. The world is as new to him as it was to the first man that existed, and his natural right in it is of the same kind.
>
> (Paine, 1995: 117)

This doctrine may not be in accordance with divine authority but it is, according to Paine, entirely in accordance with historical authority: equality is not a modern concept but 'the oldest upon record' (1995: 118).

But Paine, like other Enlightenment authors, clearly distinguished between the natural and the civil state of man. That civil state, at a first glance, appeared to have produced a rather abominable situation because what 'perhaps erroneously' is called civilization has produced 'extremes of wretchedness'; 'the most affluent and the most miserable of the human race are to be found in the countries that are called civilized' (1995: 416). Among the Indians, Paine argued,

> there is not... any of those spectacles of human misery which poverty and want present to our eyes, in all the towns and streets of Europe. Poverty, therefore, is a thing created by that which is called civilized life. It exists not in the natural state. On the other hand, the natural state is without those advantages which flow from Agriculture, Arts, Science, and Manufacture. The life of an Indian is a continual holiday, compared with the poor of Europe; and, on the other hand, it appears to be abject when compared to the rich.
>
> (Paine, 1995: 416)

Civilization, then, has produced one part of society in affluence and the other in poverty, neither of which exists in the natural state. But whereas society can always move from the natural to the civilized state, the reverse movement is not possible. This is so because

> man, in a natural state, subsisting by hunting, requires ten times the quantity of land to range over, to procure himself sustenance, than would support him in a civilized state. When therefore a country becomes populous by the additional aids of cultivation, arts, and science, there is a necessity of preserving things in that state; because without it, there cannot be sustenance for more, perhaps, than a tenth part of its inhabitants.
>
> (1995: 417)

Civilization, hence, is not possible without cultivation, argued Paine, but similarly, because civilization/cultivation can feed more people than the natural condition, its development is justified. However,

> taking then the matter up on this ground, the first principle of civilization ought to have been, and ought still to be, that the condition of every person born into the world, after a state of civilization commences, ought not to be worse than if he had been born before that period. But the fact is, that the condition of millions, in every country in Europe, is far worse than if they had been born before civilization began, or had been born among the Indians of North America of the present day.
>
> (Paine, 1995: 417)

Paine therefore concluded that

> it is a position not to be controverted, that the earth in its natural uncultivated state, was, and ever would have continued to be, the COMMON PROPERTY OF THE HUMAN RACE. In that state every man would have been born to property. He would have been a joint life-proprietor with the rest in the property of the soil, and in all its natural productions, vegetable and animal.
>
> (1995: 417)

Paine then went on to show that it was historically, indeed, the case that the first, the natural state, when men were hunters, could not produce property and neither could the second stage of development, pastoralism. Where, then, does private property come from? It emerges out of cultivation, in fact:

> from the impossibility of separating the improvement made by cultivation from the earth itself, upon which that improvement was made. The value of the improvement so far exceeded the value of the natural earth, at that time, as to absorb it; till, in the end, the common right of all became confounded into the cultivated right of the individual.
>
> (1995: 418)

Paine went on to argue that these two rights are nevertheless separate rights and proposed the introduction of a fund out of which all those members of society who have been dispossessed from their natural common ownership in the earth would receive 15 pounds sterling when they reached the age of 21 as a partial compensation for their loss of property in the land, as well as 10 pounds sterling per year as a kind of rent (1995: 419f.). The introduction of this fund, Paine argued, would take care of the negative side of civilization; it would produce more equality between the rich and the poor.

Paine, thus, reproduced classically the European position. Knowledge from which one can scientifically derive the correct, that is good and moral, principles on which society should be based is to be derived from the state of nature; to study the state of nature of mankind, one only had to study the Amerindian societies; what one could learn there was that liberty and equality were natural to man and, therefore, had to be considered natural rights of man. Common property was also natural but history had made it not only impossible but morally indefensible to return to a regime of common property because a societal organization based on common property would not produce the abundance of goods which civilized society produces. Hence, under the modern conditions of an increased population of the world, societies have to be organized on the basis of private property which is identified with agriculture and productivity. The inequalities civilization produces have to be remedied by introducing various schemes of redistribution. It is interesting to note that there is in the last instance only one element of civilization he truly defends, only one element on which his whole argument that civilization is not just materially but morally more desirable than the state of nature rests. And this element is the mode of production, it is the claim that the productivity of a civilized society depends on private property and agriculture, and that this productivity is at least theoretically capable of providing sustenance for all human beings.

There are two problems with this claim, though. The first one is that in these 'conjectures' about the state of nature the fact that most Amerindian societies actually did practise agriculture was simply denied. And this denial cannot be blamed on the difficulties of getting reliable information. In particular in North America, the English knew right from the start that the Amerindians they encountered practised agriculture – after all, the English depended on the agricultural produce of the Amerindians and even wrote reports back to England full of praise about the surplus the Amerindians produced (Williams, 1992: 211; Sheehan, 1980; Spicer, 1992; Venables, 1992: 109–11). A related difficulty lay with the idea that the universal linear development of human society would proceed along the four stages of hunting, pastoralism, agriculture, and manufacture and commerce (Meek, 1976). Indeed, the whole of America was a counter-example to this line of progression, for agriculture was very widespread in Amerindian societies whereas pastoralism was unknown and only introduced by the Europeans. The second problem, one which still haunts European societies at home and abroad, is the contradiction between ideals of equality and liberty, taken from Amerindian societies, in which these, in so far as they existed, were based on common property, and their introduction into European societies where they were combined with private property producing inequality and unfreedom. The unwillingness to draw the proper conclusions from the 'study' of Amerindian societies, to face the fact that economy, politics and social life are integrated wholes, allowed the separation of disciplines in European thought. For, now, we can leave private property to the economists and deal, in political science for instance, only with ideals like liberty and equality. And when these disciplinary lines are crossed, as we shall see in the next chapter, what we very frequently find is that contemporary authors try to solve the problem of inequality by introducing one or other redistributive scheme – exactly as Thomas Paine did. If the Enlightenment authors were right, however, in identifying the basis of liberty and equality in common property, then no amount of redistribution would solve the problem of inequality and resulting unfreedom.

If then Thomas More's *Utopia*, inspired by the discovery of Amerindian societies, travelled back to America in the luggage of Vasco de Quiroga and others who went to set up perfect Christian communities along its lines among the Amerindians, Thomas Paine demonstrates how these ideas have subsequently travelled back to Europe.

The revolution in America presented in politics what was only theory in mechanics. So deeply rooted were all the governments of the old world, and so effectually had the tyranny and the antiquity of habit established itself over the mind, that no beginning could be made in Asia, Africa, or Europe, to reform the political condition of man. Freedom had been hunted round the globe; reason was considered as rebellion; and the slavery of fear had made men afraid to think.

(Paine, 1995: 210)

Paine made it abundantly clear that the old world did, indeed, include Asia, Africa and Europe as it did for the Spaniards when they first arrived in America. And what united the old world in Paine's opinion was that governments had been erected and for a long time established on the basis of power, that reason was suppressed, and that, therefore, people in the old world did not have any kind of recollection of the true nature of man and, consequently, man's natural rights. In contrast to this condition in Europe, Asia and Africa, 'America was the only spot in the political world, where the principles of universal reformation could begin' (1995: 210). For what made America different was the fact that it presented not a picture of old and established governments, but forced people to confront nature. The early settlers in America, held Paine, came from various European nations, religions, professions. They left persecution by the European governments behind and found, in America, something 'which generates and encourages great ideas. Nature appears to him [the spectator] in magnitude' (1995: 211). The European settlers were, thus, so to speak, in the condition of the first men, for

the wants which necessarily accompany the cultivation of a wilderness produced among them a state of society, which countries, long harassed by the quarrels and intrigues of governments, had neglected to cherish. In such a situation man becomes what he ought. He sees his species, not with the inhuman idea of a natural enemy, but as kindred; and the example shews to the artificial world, that man must go back to Nature for information.

(Paine, 1995: 211)

Paine argued that the early settlers under American conditions actually developed an original, a natural society. And he thought it 'rational to conclude, that if the governments of Asia, Africa, and Europe, had begun on a principle similar to that of America, or had not been very early corrupted therefrom, that those countries must by this time have been in a far superior condition to what they are' (1995: 211). And this example of America, this opportunity to start afresh, has tremendous implications for Europe, too. For, argued Paine,

> what we now behold, may not improperly be called a *'counter-revolu-tion'*. Conquest and tyranny, at some early period, dispossessed man of his rights, and he is now recovering them. And as the tide of all human affairs has its ebb and flow in directions contrary to each other, so also is it in this. Government founded on a *moral theory, on a system of universal peace, on the indefeasible hereditary Rights of Man*, is now revolving from west to east, by a stronger impulse than the government of the sword revolved from east to west.
>
> (1995: 212f)

It was only in America, then, that Europeans could rediscover the truly natural state of man which inspired European authors to draw up blue-prints grounding society on the laws of nature; these could then first of all only and much more easily be realized in America where there were no indigenous governments to deal with and the European govern-ments were far away; but now these ideas are flowing in the opposite direction. And, thus, Paine claimed that 'the present age will hereafter merit to be called the Age of reason, and the present generation will appear to the future as the Adam of a new world' (1995: 321). In many ways, then, America signifies a new beginning for mankind, though not on new but on the original principles, the principles of creation, of nature.

And as Paine held that these ideas now flowed from West to East, from America to Europe, so he himself defended those principles, those nat-ural rights of man in the French Revolution. In September 1792, Paine was elected into the National Convention in France and, in the *Rights of Man*, defended vehemently the principles of the French Revolution against the criticism of Burke. In France, he was arrested in December 1793 and released a year later. He was welcomed back into the Conven-tion and went on publishing pamphlets in which he argued for a uni-versal (male) suffrage and for redistributive principles in taxation. On his return to America in 1802 he found the political atmosphere much changed and was attacked for his assault on Christianity. Nevertheless, Jefferson stuck by him and let him stay at the White House from where Paine continued his attacks on the Federalists. Just as Jefferson held in the Declaration of Independence that 'we hold these truths to be self evident, that all men are created equal', so Paine defended the statement in the Declaration of the Rights of Man and Citizens that 'men are born, and always continue, free, and equal in respect of their rights' and that 'the end of all political associations, is, the preservation of the natural and imprescriptible rights of man; and these rights are liberty, property, security, and resistance of oppression' (Paine, 1995: 162). These principles were, in both cases, and in line with Paine's and previous Enlightenment writers' arguments, derived from nature, a nature that had been rediscovered in America.

Paine, however, also had something to say about the international. He argued that while society itself, driven by the nature of man, produces agriculture, manufacture, commerce and the arts, the governments of Europe

> are in the same condition as we conceive of savage uncivilized life; they put themselves beyond the law as well of GOD as of man, and are, with respect to principle and reciprocal conduct, like so many individuals in a state of nature. The inhabitants of every country, under the civilization of laws, easily civilize together, but governments being yet in an uncivilized state, and almost continually at war, they pervert the abundance which civilized life produces to carry on the uncivilized part to a greater extent.
>
> (Paine, 1995: 264)

Although redistribution is one way of relieving the inequalities in civilized life, the major culprit was government. Indeed, Paine believed that as soon as all governments were based on the principles of nature and the rights of man, they would stop fighting each other and all men could benefit from civilization. Thus, it seemed enough to reform the political sphere in the narrow sense of the term, and nature – or, rather, civil society as its product – would take care of the rest. Hence, we have here an early version of the 'democracies don't fight each other thesis'. However, borrowing principles from the Amerindians whose state of nature was such a rich source of information did not mean that one did not have to defend oneself against them, for, as Paine reminds the 'Americans' in 1776, 'were the back counties to give up their arms, they would fall an easy prey to the Indians, who are all armed' (1995: 70).

Thomas Paine was not just as an individual involved in both the American and the French Revolution but he also played an important role in spreading these ideas to a general public and instigating political activities. Paine's pamphlets, clearly and passionately written, were important in the political developments at the end of the eighteenth century. Not only did he provide the American Revolution with a much broader meaning than just independence from Britain, but in Britain in the 1790s he was the most widely read pamphleteer and his works were the most often prosecuted. His was the single most successful response to Burke's *Reflections on the Revolution in France*. It instigated a revival of the extra-parliamentary reform movement in Britain and the government thought his writings so dangerous that it issued a Royal Proclamation against seditious writing in 1792 and a warrant against Paine. By this time, however, he had already gone on to France. But if this can give us some indication as to the readiness of the public not only in America and France, but also in England, to take up such ideas, the question remains where Paine had taken these ideas from. Paine himself had no formal education. He claimed that he was not indebted to others for his ideas and that, for instance, he had never read Locke. In his account, most of his ideas were taken from contemporary political controversies, newspapers and coffee house discussions in Britain, America and France. Reading Paine, it is at times difficult to believe that he had never read Locke. If his claim is genuine, then we have to conclude that by the time Paine was writing these ideas, derived from the state of nature identified with the Amerindian societies, had so strongly seeped into European culture that it was possible to distil their major elements from discussions with learned men, from newspapers, and public political debates and controversies.

During Rousseau's lifetime, his 'noble savage' still had to fight against quite a strong countercurrent in the French Enlightenment which was convinced that America in general and the Amerindian in particular was primitive and degenerate, that the climate simply would not allow for any kind of civilization and that even the white settlers degenerated over time. By 1770, however, America suddenly symbolized 'the first practical trial construction of the Heavenly City of the *Philosophes*' (Echeverría, 1956: 3, 6–13). The America of the white settlers and their political experiments came to replace the 'moribund City of God', it came to be identified with prosperity, equality, fraternity, liberty for men (1956: 24, 38). Reason and nature were substituted in the French Revolution for the Christian religion. Among the religious doctrines overthrown in this revolution was the idea of original sin from which were derived the justifications for political government as punishment. Reminiscent of Paine's Adam, the French Revolution intended to create a new man and a new world, symbolized through the introduction of the revolutionary calendar which not only replaced religion with nature in its terminology but also tradition through a new beginning, with a new Year One (Lewis, 1993: 93). Now, the original nature of man was good, it could be discovered through reason and realized in political institutions built on the nature of man, that is built on equality (Willson, 1990: 27). Salvation was now possible in this world rather than in the next. Priests and clergy were persecuted with a vengeance; if the Catholic missionaries had gone to America and destroyed Amerindian religious artifacts – or what they perceived to be religious artifacts – in the name of Christianity, they now found themselves subjected to such treatment in the name of nature. Notre Dame was rededicated to the worship of reason, God became the 'Supreme Being' whose real priest was nature, as Robespierre held, reminiscent of 'Newton's Clockmaker, Buffon's Creator of the Species, or the Freemason's Architect of the Universe' (Lewis, 1993: 96f). Liberty became a goddess and Voltaire's and Rousseau's bones were interred in the Pantheon (Willson, 1990: 31f).

If I am arguing here that the ideas derived from the state of nature have had an important impact on the politics of the American and the French Revolutions, I am, of course, not following the line of those who suggest a direct causal link, who go so far as to blame a particular author, Rousseau for instance, for the terror and violence of the French Revolution and, in extension, for the Stalinist gulags and the massacres of Pol Pot (Talmon, 1952; Tonsor, 1990: 134; Stanlis, 1990: 67f). But I will also not side with the common alternative position that the American and French Revolutions are simply to be understood as responses to particular political and economic crises, although, of course, they were that too. If I am suggesting here that the concept of the state of nature, the philosophy of history built on it, the conceptions of a perfect commonwealth and the cultural hierarchy established in the international sphere have played an important role not just in theory but also in European and North American politics, this is not an argument about direct causal effects. The development and history of this concept in European thought which I have described throughout this book has stretched over some three hundred years. It is to be understood as the adjustment and development of, arguably, a very crucial part of modern European culture. And culture, we have to remind ourselves, is not the cause of politics but its framework and meaning. The American and the French Revolutions were not 'caused' by ideas about the state of nature, but they can certainly not be understood outside the context of these cultural developments.

But this cultural context is also frequently overlooked by those who do give weight to ideas, for they tend to juxtapose the good authors and ideas with the bad ones. Thus, we find distinctions between the real Enlightenment, the good Enlightenment, and the romanticist and totalitarian, the degenerate version of it. The first is generally identified by conservative authors with the American Revolution and the second with the French Revolution. The same is done with respect to particular authors. Stanlis, for instance, counterposes Voltaire, Diderot and Burke as the good authors who did believe in reason to Rousseau, the bad one, who is emotional, a theist or pantheist (Stanlis, 1990: 63f). Tonsor, for his part, argues that Locke's theory cannot be described as a theory of radical egalitarianism and that, in accordance with Locke's understanding, the American Revolution established a highly inegalitarian and hierarchical system (Tonsor, 1990: 115, 121f). In contrast, the French Revolution did attempt to create a radically egalitarian society based on the writings, among others, of Rousseau (1990: 130). The ideology of equality based on the state of nature among the Amerindians, as Tonsor remarks, is what makes the French Revolution different from the American one. 'The republic of virtue dominated by Robespierre enacted in terrible form the equalitarian pseudo-Spartanism of Rousseau' (1990: 134). It is, of course, true that there are many and interesting differences to be discovered between the French and the American Revolutions. It is the object of this study, however, to point out the commonalities. Thus although both Stanlis and Tonsor are perfectly aware of the fact that all these authors, and not just Rousseau, rest their case on the concept of the state of nature, they present the Burkean or Lockean one as a positive example to follow, or the true Enlightenment, and denounce Rousseau's state of nature as the negative one. Thus, they miss the point that the concept of the state of nature in all its interpretations has, after the discovery of America, taken on a new, a secular, meaning. All secular orders, the Lockean, Burkean and Rousseauean, were now to be built on secular principles derived from the secular understanding of the state of nature.

And this is what, in a global context, in a context which includes other than European peoples, is the Enlightenment, is European culture at the time. That this culture is indeed quite particular and not universal becomes clear as soon as we ask ourselves how the prevelance of the right and reasonable understanding of the concept of the state of nature fared in America where the white population was, indeed, confronted with non-European peoples, even with those who were perceived to be in the state of nature and, thus, an example and empirical evidence for the natural rights to life and liberty, if not property. They did not fare well. 'Violent suppression of Indian religious practices and traditional forms of government, separation of Indian children from their homes, wholesale spoliation of treaty-guaranteed resources, forced assimilation programs, and involuntary sterilization of Indian women' represent but a few of the systematic policies which fitted very neatly into the universalist claims of the Enlightenment, Burkean, Lockean or otherwise (Williams, 1992: 325f). Presenting one internal strand of European thought or culture as negative generally goes along with representing another as positive. This strategy hides the common ground and presents us with a spurious choice, with a choice that is no choice in global terms and can certainly not claim any kind of universal validity. That Enlightenment thought has provided an extensive range of justifications for imperialism is well known. But the example of the American Revolution, based on Enlightenment principles, gives a fair warning that the 'inclusion' of different cultures into a liberal society does in no way amount to the solution of the problem of cultural difference. On the contrary, what the American experience demonstrates is precisely that universalist thought based on the state of nature cannot humanely deal with the problem of culture either nationally or internationally. And, as we shall see in the next chapter, this strategy, the strategy of juxtaposing one strand of European thought with another, is very much employed by contemporary International Relations theory.

8
Conclusion: the Consequences of the State of Nature for International Relations Theory

In this concluding chapter I will first demonstrate that the concept of the state of nature, even in its identification with 'primitive' peoples, still lies at the heart of mainstream contemporary International Relations theory. And, I will argue, it carries with it the same normative assumptions and political implications it had for classical thinkers. The implications of this case study of European political thought for the theory of International Relations, I will suggest, are to give up the concept of the state of nature.

In the last two decades of the eighteenth century, the Amerindian peoples, although still a very important source of information on the state of nature, had to share the stage with the newly discovered peoples in the Pacific, the purity of whose natural existence, unlike that of the Amerindians, had not yet been destroyed by too close contact with European nations (Meek, 1976: 215f). The state of nature, thus, was subsequently no longer identified only with the Amerindians but with 'primitive' peoples in general. And, even later, the concept of the state of nature, or the four-stage theory, had been integrated into European political thought so thoroughly that it was no longer identified with particular peoples at all. Political theory, over time, lost its awareness that there was, actually, a concrete content to the concept of the state of nature but perceived it as a 'hypothetical' concept, a theoretical device, the result of nothing but 'happenings in the head'. In light of this fact, it is remarkable how present the concrete identification of the theoretical concept of the state of nature with 'primitive' peoples still is in International Relations theory today.

Having equated the international sphere with a state of nature characterized through the absence of centralized government, we find

Morgenthau, for instance, comparing international law with the law of 'primitive' peoples, 'such as the Australian aborigines and the Yurok of Northern California' (1993: 255). In the absence of a central authority, Morgenthau argues, law can only exist either as a result of a 'community of interest' or as a result of a 'balance of power' and it is, thus, 'the result of objective social forces' (1993: 256). The same argument is made by Bull. The law of 'primitive societies' is characterized by the absence of centralized government enforcing it and, thus, has to be enforced by certain groups within society itself. It consists only of primary rules and lacks the secondary ones, the rules about rules. Hence, international law differs from municipal law 'and resembles the law of certain primitive societies' (Bull, 1977: 135f).

Another aspect of the international sphere is likened by Bull and Morgenthau to 'primitive societies', namely diplomacy. Certain very basic types of diplomacy – 'the sending of a messenger or herald, bearing his message, stick or other equivalent of letters of credence from one primitive tribe or group to a neighbouring tribe' – is a pristine form of diplomacy (Bull, 1977: 164). And even if today diplomacy is institutionalized and not just instigated for a particular event, Bull maintains, 'diplomatic contacts even among primitive peoples are often highly institutionalised in this sense, the exchange of messages and the conduct of negotiation conforming to elaborate rules backed up by magical or religious sanction' (1977: 166). For Morgenthau, because the realization of the world state is not possible under the given conditions of cultural diversity, we have to resort to those universal and timeless means of creating the conditions which will eventually make the world state possible, namely diplomacy. The basic tasks of diplomacy are, indeed, performed 'everywhere and at all times', even by 'the chieftain of a primitive tribe maintaining political relations with a neighboring tribe'; the only modern element is the fact that today they are performed by organized agencies (Morgenthau, 1993: 363). The state of nature exemplified by these 'primitive societies' provides both Bull and Morgenthau with certain general and timeless features of human life and interaction which might be used in the international sphere in order to overcome the problems generated by cultural diversity.

Similarly, we find the universal, timeless, objective features of international relations being stressed by Waltz with repeated reference to 'primitive tribes'. Waltz, for instance, rejects the assumption that without the communist threat the world could live in peace for, he states,

this recently expressed conviction is an echo of the French, British, and American chant against German militarism early in this century, of the Cobdenite chant against Russia and the Austro-Hungarian Empire in the middle of the last century, and, no doubt, of the chant of the primitive tribes against one another through many ages.
(1959: 157)

It is mistaken, he argues, to blame particular cultural, ideological, or political identities for the problems of the international sphere. Although from the perspective of mankind war might not have paid, from the perspective of 'a nation or a tribe' it might have (Waltz, 1959: 224). Insecurity in the international sphere is the automatic result of any system divided into like units, be they nations or tribes, petty principalities, empires or street gangs (1979: 67). And, furthermore, we cannot expect this problem to be overcome by, for instance, the development of the atomic bomb which some authors hope will trigger a radical change in international politics, because 'there may well have been a prophet to proclaim the end of tribal warfare when the spear was invented and another to make a similar prediction when poison was first added to its tip. Unfortunately, these prophets have all been false' (1959: 235f). In order, then, to understand the recurrence of wars between these different kinds of units, we have to abstract from the particular qualities, motives and interactions of 'tribal units' and analyse the way in which they are 'affected by tribal structure', just as if we were to analyse 'how decisions of firms are influenced by their market' (1979: 81). And for Bull, there is no question that

primitive anarchical societies clearly have important resemblances to international society in respect to the maintenance of order. In both cases some element of order is maintained despite the absence of a central authority commanding overwhelming force and a monopoly of the legitimate use of it. In both cases, also, this is achieved through the assumption by particular groups – lineage and locality groups in primitive stateless societies, sovereign states in international society – of the functions which, in a modern state, the government (but not the government exclusively) carries out in making rules effective. ... In primitive anarchical societies, as in international society, the relations between these politically competent groups are themselves circumscribed by a structure of acknowledged normative principles, even at times of violent struggle. But in both there is a tendency, during these periods of struggle, for the structure of rules to break down, and the society to fall apart to such an extent that the warring tribes or states are better described as a number of contending societies than as a single society. Finally, in both primitive anarchical society and modern international society there are factors operating, outside the structure of rules itself, inducing the politically competent groups to conform to them.

(Bull, 1977: 62)

This is not to say, though, that Bull does not also see differences between 'primitive' anarchical societies and international society. He notes that modern states have exclusive rights to territory and supreme jurisdiction over their citizens; they tend to be more self-sufficient and self-regarding; the modern states system is culturally heterogeneous while 'primitive' societies are culturally homogeneous; the former is secular while the latter has a common religion; and there is a difference in size between them (1977: 63–5). Bull concludes that 'primitive' anarchical societies demonstrate much more cohesion than the modern states system (1977: 65). Notwithstanding these differences, we can learn a lot about international relations by looking at 'primitive anarchical societies'. In this theoretical exposition, Bull stresses the fact that these 'primitive societies' do clearly exhibit and reproduce order and, therefore, in so far as they are similar to the international society the latter is also characterized by some kind of order (1977: 61). The state of nature, 'tribes', 'primitive peoples', then, are indeed very much present in International Relations theory. And, in the above mentioned examples, their function is always the same: the analysis of 'tribal life' or 'primitive peoples' can tell us something about the underlying, real 'nature' of the international sphere as opposed to its culturally diverse surface appearance, and it provides us with certain 'tools' like 'primitive law' or diplomacy which in their timelessness seem to be part of human nature and at the disposal of any society at any time, even such a 'primitive' society as the contemporary international one.

And, indeed, the same is true for the Liberals. Hoffman, for instance, identifies the international system with a 'jungle' that has to be turned into a society (1981: 35). Not only is the 'jungle' morally inferior to 'society', but there is also a clear moral hierarchy between different kinds of societies because 'if (as in primitive societies) integration is total, there is no moral choice at all' (Hoffman, 1981: 35). Hence, the extent of cultural integration – homogeneity in Bull's terms – in 'primitive societies' does not allow for moral choices. Nevertheless, the values underlying a true society, one in which moral choices are possible and into which, therefore, the international 'jungle' has to be transformed, are for the Liberals, too, taken from the state of nature. For, the belief that individuals have human rights 'that derive from their *nature*' – such as the right to strive for the good life, the right to personal and moral fulfillment – implies that society has to be organized in such a way as to make the fulfillment of these rights possible; and these rights, because they are derived from the *nature* of human beings cannot be restricted to domestic jurisdiction but cut across 'the deep cultural, social, and political differences that underlie mankind's division' (Hoffman, 1981: 109; emphasis added).

Among these fundamental rights, in the eyes of the Liberals, are liberty, equality and the right to private property (Doyle, 1983: 207). And these Liberal principles are based on an understanding of human nature, for

> Liberals assume individuals to be both self-interested and rationally capable of accomodating their conflicting interests. They have held that principles such as rule under law, majority rule, and the protection of private property that follow from mutual accommodation among rational, self-interested people are the best guide to present policy.
>
> (Doyle, 1983: 348f)

And Beitz, even though he cannot tell us what universal justice in concrete terms will consist of (1979: 122), and thus leaves 'a gaping hole at the heart of his theory', as Hoffman has pointed out (1981: 57), clearly states how we can arrive at a conception of universal justice. With respect to the rights of states as well as with respect to distributive justice, Beitz holds with Kant that 'our justification of normative principles must appeal ultimately to those kinds of considerations that are appropriate in a prescriptive context, namely, the rights and interests of persons', in other words, only individuals can be the end of moral actions (Beitz, 1979: 53). Moral principles, he holds, cannot be derived from a state of nature between states but have to be derived from an individual state of nature which is 'the common foundation of principles in both realms' (1979: 63). This individual state of nature, or Rawlsian original position, is based on the idea of a 'hypothetical social contract' in which we have to 'imagine rational persons' under conditions which exclude 'knowledge about the particular identities and interests of the parties, their generation and place in society, and their society's history, level of development, and culture' (1979: 130). Reason, then, is universal, it is part of the nature of human beings and can clearly transcend any historical, social, political and cultural identity. If 'primitive societies' left no doubt in the minds of the Realists that diplomacy and 'primitive' forms of law were part of human nature and, therefore, detectable through reason, Liberals discovered with that same natural reason certain universally valid principles of societal organiza-tion, domestic and international, in the nature of man. Those are, generally, liberty, equality of opportunity, and private property (Doyle, 1983: 207; Hoffman, 1981: 109; Beitz 77–9, 141).

The principles of establishing valid knowledge, then, are still the same as they were for the Enlightenment writers. That is, one presupposes human nature as distinct from culture which can then either be studied among 'primitive peoples' or 'imagined' as a 'hypothetical condition'. And from this state of nature, either real or imagined, one can derive principles for the political and social organization of mankind, domestic and international. It is not too surprising, then, that the principles derived from this state of nature are also still the same as they were for the Enlightenment writers. What is rather disconcerting, though, is the fact that quite frequently contemporary authors are blissfully unaware of the fact that they are not just reinventing the wheel but, rather more seriously, justifying in the process the very policies which have pro-duced injustice and inequality in the international sphere in the first place. Charles Beitz's principles of redistributive justice are a prime example for this.

Going back to the individual, Beitz argues that natural resources, like individual talents, are not deserved. But, whereas talents are 'naturally attached to persons', resources are found 'out there', available to the 'first taker' (Beitz, 1979: 139). Talents, then, are an integral part of an individual's identity to which the individual, therefore, has a natural right, while people do not have natural rights to resources. Resources 'must first be appropriated, and prior to their appropriation, no one has any special natural claim on them' (1979: 140). In the original interna-tional position, Beitz elaborates, the parties would know that resources are unevenly distributed, that access to resources is necessary for suc-cessful domestic societies, that resources are scarce, but they would not know the resource endowments of their own societies. Hence, they would agree on a distributive principle allowing every society

a fair chance to develop just political institutions and an economy capable of satisfying its members' basic needs. There is no intuitively obvious standard of equity for such matters; perhaps the standard would be population size, or perhaps it would be more complicated, rewarding societies for their members' efforts in extracting resources and taking account of the different resource needs of societies with different economies. The underlying principle is that each person has an equal prima facie claim to a share of the total available resources.

(Beitz, 1979: 141)

What we are confronted with, here, is a perfect reproduction of the arguments which the classical European authors made for the expropriation of, for instance, the Amerindian peoples. That is, the overpopulation in Europe and the abundance of land in America justified a redistribution in favour of the Europeans; so, too, the Europeans were entitled to American land because their economic system extracted more resources and produced more than the Amerindian societies. Most importantly, however, this redistribution in favour of the Europeans was justified with reference to the (potential) benefits of each and every individual member of humanity; that is, the Amerindian mode of production did not produce the abundance to feed more than the members of their own societies, while the European mode of production would benefit all of humanity by producing a surplus which could be redistributed. This redistribution, obviously, was not all that effective, for otherwise neither Beitz nor Doyle or Hoffman would have to write extensively on the need for a new or more effective principle for redistribution, just as Thomas Paine had done. There is no doubt that Beitz's attempt to extend the Rawlsian principles of justice, derived from an original position or state of nature, to the international sphere is meant as a radical and critical contribution. Precisely because of this intention it is all the more tragic that he ends up not just reproducing but, more importantly, justifying exactly those arguments of the classical writers who, with reference to the good of all human beings, have denied non-Europeans equal rights.

However, mainstream International Relations theory does also reproduce a philosophy of history based on the concept of the state of nature. This philosophy of history rests on the assumption that the state of nature, despite the fact that it provides universally valid principles, also has disadvantages compared with the modern state. Hence, Morgenthau argues that although the state is not the only feature necessary, it is nevertheless 'indispensable for the maintenance of domestic peace' and 'society has no substitute for the power of the Leviathan' (1993: 339). State-building is not just necessary but also positive because it sets limits to the struggle for power which is universal in time and space, which is part of those 'bio-psychological drives... to live, to propagate, and to dominate' which according to Morgenthau are basic features of human nature and, thus, create society (Morgenthau, 1993: 36f). Although the drive for power is universal in time and space no society can actually live by it. All societies have to regulate and channel these power drives in order to protect the weak from the powerful and so 'morality, mores, and law' are an inherent part of the human condition; human beings are moral beings by virtue of their humanity (1993: 220, 249).

The successful story of Western civilization 'from the Bible to the ethics and constitutional arrangements of modern democracy' is that its 'ethics, mores, and legal systems' recognize and condemn these drives for power (1993: 219f). The West has played a particularly progressive role, according to Morgenthau, in developing those moral rules which regulate the universal drive for power.

> The best that Western civilization has been able to achieve – which is, as far as we can see, *the best that any civilization can achieve* – has been to mitigate the struggle for power on the domestic scene, to civilize its means, and to direct it toward objectives that, if attained, minimize the extent to which life, liberty, and the pursuit of happiness of the individual members of society are involved in the struggle for power.
>
> (Morgenthau, 1993: 223; emphasis added)

Western civilization, he argues, has replaced the crude and violent methods of personal combat with 'refined instruments of social, commercial, and professional competition' like competitive examinations, competition for social distinctions, competition for public offices, and, in particular, 'with competition for the possession of money' (1993: 223). The competition for money is, in Morgenthau's reading, the civilized substitute for the natural drive to power which makes possible the normative injunctions against individual and collective violence. Bearing in mind that even Morgenthau assumes that all societies have to regulate these drives for power in various different ways, it appears that the competition for money is taken by him to constitute the most civilized and successful method developed by humankind so far.

However, this successful pacification, domestification and civilization which Western societies have achieved internally has clearly had an adverse effect on international relations. For, on the one hand, the ever increasing homogenization of the national community went hand in hand with the dissolution of a wider political unity, Christendom, and the erection of sovereign states within that formerly more unified realm, 'as the rise of the territorial state transformed the Holy Roman Empire from the actual political organization of Christendom into an empty shell and a legal fiction' (Morgenthau, 1993: 277, 253f). On the other hand, the rise of the nation-state and the exclusive national loyalties of the population led to a demise in the moral unity which underpinned that earlier, wider, and more universalist morality and to the development of what Morgenthau calls nationalistic universalism, that is, the belief that one's own morality, rules and institutions are universally valid and should be taken on by all the other communities in the international realm (1993: 272f). There is no doubt for Morgenthau that all the 'supranational forces' which tie people together across boundaries are 'infinitely weaker today' than those that separate them; this development is 'the negative by-product of the great positive force that shapes the political face of our age – nationalism' (1993: 272).

As a result of this development, what we witness today, is that 'increasing homogenization and pacification of life within the state' brings with it simultaneously in the international sphere a regression to the 'morality of tribalism, of the Crusades, and of the religious wars' (1993: 245). Although Morgenthau clearly links these two adverse developments, he holds on to the belief that Western civilization distinguishes itself from others since the time of the Stoics and early Christians through the striving for a political organization commensurate with 'the moral unity of mankind' (1993: 277f). In this striving for the moral unity of mankind inherent in Western civilization, the philosophy of the Enlightenment and the theory of liberalism, exemplified by Kant and Diderot occupy, according to Morgenthau, an honourable, if eventually fruitless position (1993: 278). For what these Liberal writers overlook, he argues, is not only that in the international sphere that bond which unites the members of a domestic society does not exist, but even that the progress of domestic society with respect to morality itself confounds the problems of the international in that the belief in the universal validity of the domestic values leads to the 'moral duty to punish and to wipe off the face of the earth the professors and practitioners of evil' (1993: 233f). But this does not mean, according to Morgenthau, that one cannot or should not strive for world peace; rather it means that one first has to establish the conditions, trust and moral bonds, which are the preconditions for a world state and the method by which this can be done 'we will call peace through accommodation. Its instrument is diplomacy' (1993: 361).

In this philosophy of history we encounter the same normative judgements that the classical writers made. The domestic development of Western civilization appears as the most progressive moral and political development in the world. In comparison with the state of nature, it is the institution of government in combination with a culture devoted to the idea of the moral unity of mankind which has made possible those ultimate heights of domestic pacification. And just as for de Tocqueville the extermination of the indigenous population did not invalidate the American experiment necessarily, so too, for Morgenthau, the fact that his account of domestic development is inextricably linked to a moral and political regression in international relations does not relativize his positive evaluation of Western political thought and practice. This contradiction, implicit in Western culture, is not to be overcome by a re-evaluation of Western culture, it is to be overcome by a return to the nature of human beings and, consequently, the timeless nature of their social life which provides us with instruments like diplomacy, neutral or natural instruments in order to overcome the cultural division of the world. What Morgenthau does not realize, precisely because he starts out with the assumption that state-building is not just natural but also positive, is that European state-building itself was justified over and against different kinds of political communities to whom the rights of Western states did not have to be extended. It is, then, not the case that the international sphere is automatically devoid of moral obligations. Rather, the international sphere has been deliberately constructed as such and this construction is itself a moral act – it is not given in the nature of things. It is the result of Western moral theory and political practice. But Morgenthau, of course, is not an exception but the rule.

The modern Western state is for Bull, too, clearly an advance on earlier forms of political organization. 'Primitive societies', he states, do have a kind of law but this law consists only of primary rules and it lacks the secondary rules which modern Western states have developed. And although it is possible for a society to live by primary rules alone, this has certain defects because 'these rules will have a *static* character; there will be no means of deliberately adapting the rules to changing circumstances, by eliminating old rules or introducing new ones'; in addition, in the absence of secondary rules, some 'disputes are likely to continue interminably' and, if any doubt should arise, there is no way to determine what the rules are (Bull, 1977: 134f). A society which lives by primary rules only is necessarily a static society; it is also inefficient, and it might deteriorate into interminable conflicts; in short, primitive societies are very much like the state of nature the Enlightenment writers had identified: stagnant, inefficient, without progress, forever warring.

The absence of government, too, in 'primitive societies' has negative implications, for

> the development of the modern concept of war as organised violence among sovereign states was the outcome of a process of limitation or confinement of violence. We are accustomed, in the modern world, to contrast war between states with peace between states; but the historical alternative of war between states was more ubiquitous violence ... [Historically,] war is very often not the servant of rational or intelligent purposes; it has been fought by primitive tribes as a form of ritual, by Christian and Saracen Knights in fulfilment of a chivalric code, by modern states to test their cohesion and sense of identity, and throughout history from sheer lust for blood and conquest.
>
> (Bull, 1977: 185–6)

Hence, the modern state can be seen as an advance in the sense that it has suppressed violence amongst its population on the one hand, and in the sense of using war in the international system according to rules of law on the other. That is, although war is taken to be a threat to international society, it also is 'a means of enforcing international law, of preserving the balance of power, and, arguably, of promoting changes in the law generally regarded as just' (1977: 187f). The third element with respect to which modern states can be regarded as an advance is the 'stabilisation of possession by rules of property' (1977: 18f). Just as in the writings of the early international lawyers, Bull points out that the recognition of property is reflected in the acceptance of sovereignty which 'derived historically from the idea that certain territories and peoples were the property or patrimony of the ruler', and, we recall, sovereignty based on property was supposed to end wars over common resources (1977: 19).

Bull, then, also identifies the institution of the modern state, and in particular its domestic organization, as a morally and politically progressive development. However, for Bull, too, the international sphere does show more of an adverse development. Whereas natural law thinkers still expressed a sense of the moral unity of mankind, the development of the state and the replacement of natural law by positive international law clearly reduced the sense of moral responsibility which Europeans felt towards non-European peoples (1977: 28–35f).

And in the nineteenth century we are confronted with a clear hierarchy of cultures as the basis for European thought about international relations which was expressed in the orthodox doctrine that 'mankind was divided into civilised humanity, barbarous humanity and savage humanity' (1977: 38). And Bull points out that this distinction is in fact 'the same one which is made by social scientists today when they distinguish between modern societies, traditional societies and primitive societies' (1977: 38). For Bull, historically

> the revolt of non-European peoples and states against Western dominance, and the expansion of the states system beyond its originally European or Western confines, have produced an international system in which the area of consensus has shrunk by comparison with what it was in 1914.... Indeed, the international history of this century so far may be regarded as a prolonged attempt to cope with the drastic decline of the element of society in international relations...
>
> (Bull, 1977: 258)

Meanwhile Waltz, although he does not comment on history very much, takes on board Rousseau's philosophy of history. In the state of nature, which is also the condition states find themselves in in the international sphere, Waltz argues,

> men are governed by 'instinct', 'physical impulses', 'right of appetite'; and 'liberty... bounded only by the strength of the individual.' Agreements cannot bind, for 'in default of natural sanctions, the laws of justice are ineffective among men.' Without the protection of civil law, even agriculture is impossible, for who, Rousseau asks, 'would be so absurd as to take the trouble of cultivating a field, which might be stripped of its crop by the first comer?' To be provident is impossible, for without social regulation there can be no obligation to respect the interests, rights, and property of others.
>
> (Waltz, 1959: 171f)

But this state of nature is not, in the last instance, considered to be positive, for although 'it is society that is the degrading force in men's lives... it is the moralizing agency as well. And this latter effect Rousseau was unwilling to surrender even had he thought it possible for men to retreat to the state of nature' (Waltz, 1959: 4f). State-building is, indeed, justified and a solution to that kind of life which, among other disadvantages, does not make possible the material production to feed an increased population (1959: 167). In the state of nature 'to be provident is impossible, for without social regulation there can be no obligation to respect the interests, rights, and property of others. But to be provident is desirable, for it makes life easier; or even necessary, for population begins to press on the amount of food available under a given mode of production'; in addition, however, state-building is also the basis for morality

> by substituting justice for instinct in his [man's] conduct, and giving his actions the morality they had formerly lacked. Man prior to the establishment of the civil state possesses natural liberty; he has a right to all he can get. This natural liberty he abandons when he enters the civil state. In return he receives 'civil liberty and the proprietorship of all he possesses.' Natural liberty becomes civil liberty; possession becomes proprietorship. And in addition 'man acquires in the civil state, moral liberty, which alone makes him truly master of himself; for the mere impulse of appetite is slavery, while obedience to a law which we prescribe to ourselves is liberty'.
>
> (Waltz, 1959: 171f)

By ascribing morality as such to citizens who live in states, it is implicitly denied to those peoples who choose other forms of political organization; they live by instinct and natural impulse rather than by reason and morality.

> The argument is clear. For individuals the bloodiest stage of history was the period just prior to the establishment of society. At that point they had lost the virtues of the savage without having acquired those of the citizen. The late stage of the state of nature is necessarily a state of war. The nations of Europe are precisely in that stage.
>
> (Waltz, 1959: 184)

But despite the fact that here, again, state-building simply means that the individual state of nature with all its disadvantages and, in particular, with the absence of morality, is simply exported into the international realm, this development is nevertheless justified, for 'the state of nature among men is a monstrous impossibility. Anarchy breeds war among them, government establishes the conditions for peace. The state of nature that continues to prevail among states often produces monstrous behavior but so far has not made life itself impossible' (1959: 227f). In other words, what we gain through the pacification of domestic society through the state clearly outweighs what we might lose in the international sphere.

Liberals, too, stress the progressive character of certain domestic developments in Western or liberal states. Just like the Realists, Hoffman holds that Western political philosophy and liberalism are nothing else but the attempt to develop a morality along the lines of Locke, Rousseau, and Kant which combines the good of the nation with that of the rest of humanity (Hoffman, 1981: 24). And like them, he too thinks that there was a time in European history when princes were bound together by a common notion of legitimacy – even if they did not always act accordingly – and that this time has long past given way to self-righteousness (1981: 19, 50). Despite the domestic progress in Liberal societies,

> the international system is much more heterogeneous than at any other moment; not only in terms of ideologies, but also in the sense that there is a radical difference between states run by secular churches, where power rests on a kind of fusion of physical control and legitimizing dogma, and all the others, or in the sense that states behave as if they did belong to different ages of international affairs. The new states which have just acceded at least to the appearance of sovereignty have a way of acting as if state behavior of the eighteenth and nineteenth centuries was still the norm...
>
> (Hoffman, 1981: 201)

The norm, hence, is the behaviour of the Western, secularized states. But, in any case, while the domestic organization of the Western states has clearly developed progressively, the international at the same time, and for related reasons, has developed in the opposite direction. That is, from a situation of cultural or religious relative homogeneity into one of extreme cultural heterogeneity, the scene is crowded with newcomer states who are, nevertheless, in their behaviour clearly backward. And for Doyle, liberal states have not just progressed internally, but even in the international realm where they have been able to keep peace among themselves for almost two hundred years (Doyle, 1983: 217). Doyle and Hoffman, interestingly enough, do not only recognize the contradictory development between domestic and international relations, but even point out that these contradictory developments might have something to do with the liberal principles themselves. Hoffman argues that the civil and political rights, the rights to life and liberty, might come into conflict with the economic rights, that is with the right to property

(Hoffman, 1981: 104). He uses the relatively optimistic metaphor of a circle turning into a spiral with respect to the future of political human rights in the international system, yet compares the problem of distributive justice with Sisyphus and his rock. 'If death defines the human condition, injustice defines the social one. There is a duty, national and international, to reduce it as much as possible. But there is no definitive victory' (1981: 187). We note with interest that social injustice has suddenly become part of the natural condition of man, whereas the Enlightenment writers had, indeed, derived the principle of social equality – and not just equality before the law – from the state of nature.

Doyle, too, realizes that the failure of liberal states to keep peace with non-liberal states is to be sought in the contradictory principles on which Liberalism rests. Liberal states have, historically, holds Doyle, developed a crusading foreign policy with respect to non-liberal states. 'Respecting a nonliberal state's state rights to noninterference requires ignoring the violations of rights they inflict on their own populations. Addressing the rights of individuals in the Third World requires ignoring the rights of states to be free of foreign intervention' (Doyle, 1983: 330). Both these rights, those of states and those of individuals are part of the liberal theory. 'A liberal imperialism that promotes liberalism neither abroad nor at home was one result of this dilemma. Protecting "native rights" from "native" oppressors, and protecting universal rights of property and settlement from local transgressions, introduced especially liberal motives for imperial rule' (1983: 331). While there was a lot of progress to be reported from the domestic development of liberal states, 'the protection of cosmopolitan liberal rights thus bred a demand for imperial rule that violated the equality of American Indians, Africans, and Asians. In practice, once the exigencies of ruling an empire came into play, liberal imperialism resulted in the oppression of "native" liberals seeking self-determination in order to maintain imperial security...' (1983: 332).

Thus, Doyle and Hoffman put their finger on exactly that contradiction which the Enlightenment writers have produced when they attempted to combine the ideals of liberty and equality, supposedly found in Amerindian societies, with the institution of private property and state-building developed by European societies. This particular contradiction is indeed a crucial one, for it demonstrates beautifully the consequences of separating nature and culture. The social equality found in Amerindian communities was part of a cultural system combining a particular form of interaction between human beings with a particular form of interaction between them and nature. The social and political equality found in (some) Amerindian communities only existed in combination with their mode of production based on common property (in land). The same is, of course, true for any other cultural system including the European one: that is, social relations, political organization and production are combined in a systematic and culturally specific way. When Europeans separated nature from culture, in effect they perceived the social and political organization of humanity as abstractable from its interaction with nature, production. European societies have, indeed, been bedevilled by this tension between the way in which they, ideally, organize the relations between human beings, namely as equal and free, and the way in which they organize production, namely unequally on the basis of private property. This also explains not just the obsession but also the failure of the liberal schemes of redistribution. For redistribution among human beings without the reorganization of production, of human interaction with nature, is bound to fail. Hoffman has indeed seen this, when he argues that questions of human rights only deal with the surface appearance, the symptoms, whereas the causes of injustice lie in 'the nature of political regimes and economic systems' (Hoffman, 1981: 141). But, as we have seen above, this insight does not lead him to reconsider the principles derived from nature in light of their cultural coherence. He would rather read social injustice back into nature than to reintegrate nature and culture.

And this is true for the way in which both Liberals and Realists deal with the contradictions they clearly recognize. For Realists, the institution of the state itself, and for Liberals the institution and development of states embodying liberal principles are derived from the state of nature and, therefore, are valid for all of humanity. The negative international effects do not lead to a reconsideration of the positive judgement of statehood or liberal statehood because, as nature is separated from culture, so is theory from practice. The internal contradictions of the liberal principles and the mixed historical record of liberalism does not lead Doyle to ground foreign policy on any other than a liberal understanding of human nature. On the contrary, 'liberal policies thus must attempt to promote liberal principles abroad: to secure basic human needs, civil rights, and democracy, and to expand the scope and effectiveness of the world market economy'; indeed, Doyle holds, 'the goal of concerned liberals must be to reduce the harmful impact of the dilemmas without undermining the successes' (1983: 344). And so, too, Hoffman and Beitz find potential benefits in the practice of colonialism. For if colonial rule should consist of the 'provision of social infrastructure, agricultural development, education and technology', then we have to assume that 'rational members of a subject group would choose them' (Beitz, 1979: 100). Meanwhile, Hoffman finds it difficult to weigh the positive colonial provision of 'law and order' against such evils as the destruction of native communities and institutions, of self-respect, or the perception of exploitation 'far beyond the actual provable economic exploitation' (Hoffman, 1981: 159). Thus, agriculture and technology, which even for the classical thinkers made Western societies morally better than others and justified the non-extension of equal rights to the latter's communities, are naturally 'rational', whereas Hoffman clearly believes that law and order can be separated from other institutions and from economic exploitation and weighed on a different scale.

Thus far we have seen that both Realists and Liberals derive their respective theories of International Relations from the concept of the state of nature, and both also share the philosophy of history derived from this state of nature. So, too, they share with each other and with the classical writers the assumption of a hierarchy of cultures which, in fact, are subject to different kinds of rights. Although it is clearly the case that Realists emphasize state-building as such, in the last instance, their justification of the state is derived from a universal state of nature between individuals. This is an aspect of Realism which Liberals frequently prefer to overlook when they accuse Realism of accepting states' rights and, thus, tolerating or prolonging the immoral character of international politics. At the same time, Liberals frequently downplay their own justification of the state. For, while they emphasize the individual rights derived from the state of nature, they nevertheless also extend rights to states. It is, then, not the case that states can never claim any rights, 'but rather that such a right, when it exists, is a derivative of more basic principles of justice', namely those derived from the individual state of nature (Beitz, 1979: 69). That is, in the international realm only those states can claim the right to non-interference 'whose institutions conform to appropriate principles of justice and those whose institutions are more likely to become just in the absence of outside interference than with outside assistance' (1979: 90). Thus, we are confronted with two types of states, states which are either 'just, or... likely to become just if left free from external interference' (1979: 91). And then there is a third type of state which 'is neither just nor likely to become just' and which, therefore, cannot claim the right to non-interference (1979: 92).

Hoffman is much more cautious than Beitz. But he, too, suggests a foreign policy with regard to human rights, for instance, which respects the rights of some states and not those of others, depending on their cultural traditions as well as their economic and institutional level of development (Hoffman, 1981: 121). What Hoffman proposes is a 'common floor', that is, the prevention of the most atrocious human rights violations, and a 'movable ceiling', that is, a policy which demands compliance with universal human rights based on human nature in correlation with the level of development of any given country (1981: 121f). Thus, for Hoffman, too, states in the international sphere are ranked according to their cultural, economic and institutional development, and he suggests the application of different kinds of foreign policy to states on different levels of development. Similarly for Doyle there are three different types of states which will have to be treated differently, so that, 'once the Realists set a prudent policy toward the USSR, the liberals can then take over again, defining more supportive and interdependent policies toward those countries more liberal than the USSR, and more constraining and more containing policies toward countries less liberal than the USSR' (Doyle, 1983: 345). What this means is that the world is divided into three spheres, the first being the pacific union of the liberal states, the second those countries that are fairly close or show some promise of becoming liberal if they are not disaffected by contradictory and hypocritical liberal foreign policies (countries more liberal than the USSR), and the third, those which are far away from liberal ideals and, therefore, have to be treated with constraining and containing policies.

There is, then, nothing much to choose either theoretically or practically between Realism and Liberalism. Despite their protestations of the 'immorality' of Realism, as we have just seen, Liberals do not only also justify states' rights – if only those of certain kinds of states – but they are quite happy, and have been in the past, to accept Realist policies, that is, the application of force, against those states who are first, not living up to the liberal principles, and second, not powerful enough to retaliate. Thus, Hoffman combines realist and liberal principles in his foreign policy advice just as clearly as Doyle does, for he argues that states have two kinds of moral ends: self-regarding ends and other-regarding ends. In order to live up to the first category, states have to advance and protect the long-term interests of the national community; and in order to live up to the second category, they have to protect the rights of foreign states as well as the rights of individuals throughout the world (Hoffman, 1981: 190). In other words, there is a moral justification for

any kind of policy – protecting domestic or foreign individuals, defending one's own or foreign states, or the rules of the society of states...

Culture, then, exerts quite a considerable power in mainstream International Relations. For the concept of the state of nature contains a culturally peculiar understanding of human nature, history, and destiny. However, since it hides the concrete historical contents and context in which it has been developed and validates the production of knowledge on the basis of 'natural' principles distinct from and in contrast to cultural practice, it is no longer open to examination and reflection. Thus, Liberal and Realist theories of International Relations are doomed to reproduce the theory and practice of hundreds of years of European international politics. They explain the 'nature' of the international with reference to 'primitive societies' in the state of nature, or with reference to a 'hypothetical' state of nature; they derive from this state of nature various universally valid principles which happen to define European forms of state formation and domestic political organization as morally superior to those of other peoples; on the basis of these principles, they rank the different cultures of this world and apply different moral and legal principles to them; and even when they are aware of the contradictions between their principles and the historical practice, they cannot escape these contradictions in any other way but to read them back into human nature.

The discipline of International Relations, though, is neither alone in this dilemma nor worse than other disciplines. For, as we have seen, all the modern disciplines in social thought have their origin in those classical writers who developed the concept of the state of nature in its modern sense. The discipline of International Relations, however, is particularly well placed to escape this dilemma. For it is the only discipline whose subject matter, by definition, is the conditions of cooperation and conflict between different cultures. If, as I have suggested in this study, culture is constitutive of human nature rather than a deviation from it, the discipline of International Relations would do well to abolish the concept of the state of nature and the theories based on it. If human beings, in their interaction with each other as well as with their natural environment, depend on culture which organizes, directs and gives meaning to these activities in specific ways, if there is no human nature without culture, then theories of International Relations too must be constructed on that basis. Such a theory of International Relations could return to the fact which mainstream International Relations theory, as I have shown at the beginning of this book, has identified as a defining feature of the international, namely a world of different cultures. Only this time, it would enquire into the conditions of cooperation and conflict between cultures which are mutually constitutive and subject to change, rather than hope for the day when nature will eventually overcome culture.

Notes

Chapter 1   Culture, Nature and the Ambivalence of International Theory

1   Hans Morgenthau, for instance, uses the term culture in various different contexts and with various different meanings. Discussing the project of Unesco to facilitate the establishment of a world community through cultural exchange and understanding he uses the term culture, firstly, meaning cultural products or artefacts like the writings of Shakespeare or Russian musical compositions (1993: 350f.), secondly, in the sense of different communities either having or not having much culture – such as the Germans being highly educated and steeped in classical culture as opposed to primitive peoples 'completely lacking in institutionalized education... and receptive to the influence of foreign cultures to the point of suicide' (1993: 350), thirdly, as defining different phases in the historical development of humankind (1993: 11), while fourthly, there are different national cultures persistent over time such as German militarism, American indecisive pragmatism etc. (1993: 144f.), to mention but a few of the meanings of culture.

2   Morgenthau, Bull, and Waltz can be taken as a representative sample of Realist thought for two reasons. Firstly, they represent different strands of Realism: Morgenthau traditional or classical Realism, Bull the so-called English school or liberal Realism, and Waltz neo- or structural Realism. Secondly, these three authors have written systematic and comprehensive studies – *Politics Among Nations*, *The Anarchical Society*, *Man, the State, and War* and *Theory of International Politics* – setting out their theoretical conception of the international which are widely used as starting points for understanding as well as elaborating on Realist thought.

3   The Liberal authors I will concentrate on are Charles Beitz, Stanley Hoffman and Michael Doyle. As in the case of the Realists, these three authors represent methodologically as well as in their positions different strands of Liberal thought.

4   Although Beitz claims in a footnote that his arguments do not depend on the claim that interdependence is something new, he repeatedly formulates the position that Realist conceptions captured the international more accurately in the past then they do now, and that it is the contemporary development of empirical international relations which makes universal moral norms possible or necessary (Beitz, 1979: 4n., 35f., 40, 128, 132).

5   These are the two Rawlsian principles of justice, the first of which states that every individual has to have an equal right to basic liberties compatible with the same liberties for others (the political rights); the second principle states that social and economic inequalities are to be distributed in such a way that the least advantaged have the greatest benefit (the economic rights).

Chapter 4   The Politics of the State of Nature in the 'New' World

1 For these reasons, the Inquisition did not have any jurisdiction over the Amerindians (Parry, 1990: 175).

Chapter 5   The Tyranny of the European Context: Reading Classical Political Theory in International Relations

1 My interpretation is, of course, not altogether new. There are a number of authors who have seen and elaborated exactly those points which I am going to make. There is considerable overlap, for instance, between my own and Ronald Meek's study (1976) not only in terms of the range of authors he analyses but also in terms of the major thrust of the argument. Meek, however, concentrates on the emergence and development of the four-stage theory which played such an important role in the writings of classical political economists and he juxtaposes the image of the 'ignoble savage' as the basis of this theory to the image of the 'noble savage' which played a more prominent role in classical political theory, whereas I am arguing that both the 'noble' and 'ignoble' savage, that is man in the state of nature as a combination of 'noble' and 'ignoble' traits, play a constitutive role for the development of modern European social and political thought and its subsequent separation into different disciplines like political theory, political economy and international relations. A very similar argument is also put forward in the writings of Anthony Pagden (1993, 1990, 1982) as well as in those of Urs Bitterli (1982) and John Parry (1981), to mention but a few. What all these authors have in common is that they systematically analyse the influence of the international – non-European – on the European development, rather than following the conventional reverse line of argument. However, none of them analyses the impact of these developments on the discipline of International Relations, as I do in this study.

Chapter 6   The State of Nature as the Basis for Classical Political Thought

1 Even though the text is published under Raynal's name only (Abbé Raynal, *Philosophical and Political History of the Settlements and Trade of the Europeans in the East and West Indies*, New York: Negro University Press, 1969), I will speak of Raynal and Diderot because Diderot edited and added major parts of the text, in particular the passages including a moral assessment of the political history.
2 This is Christian Thomasius' introduction to the German translation of Grotius.
3 The encounter with the Amerindians is, of course, not the only source for the concept of linear historical time. However, the authors quoted here develop their philosophy of history *expressis verbis* on the assumption of a state of nature directly linked to the Amerindians.

Bibliography

Aston, Margaret (1986) *The Fifteenth Century. The Prospect of Europe*. London: Thames & Hudson.

Axtell, James (1975) 'The European Failure to Convert the Indians: An Autopsy', in *National Museum of Man*, Mercury Series, Ottawa.

Bacon, Francis (1996) *Francis Bacon. A Critical Edition of the Major Works*, ed. Brian Vickers. Oxford: Oxford University Press.

Beitz, Charles R. (1979) *Political Theory and International Relations*. Princeton, NJ: Princeton University Press.

Bitterli, Urs (1982) *Die 'Wilden' und die 'Zivilisierten'. Die europäisch-überseeische Begegnung*. Munich: Deutscher Taschenbuch Verlag.

Boucher, David (1998) *Political Theories of International Relations*. Oxford: Oxford University Press.

Bull, Hedley (1977) *The Anarchical Society. A Study of Order in World Politics*. New York: Columbia University Press.

Campanella, Tommaso (1981) *The City of the Sun: A Poetical Dialogue*. Berkeley: University of California Press.

Canning, Joseph (1996) *A History of Medieval Political Thought 300–1450*. London: Routledge.

Carr, E. H. (1981) *The Twenty Years' Crisis*. London: Macmillan.

Chiapelli, Fredi (ed.) (1976) *First Images of America. The Impact of the New World on the Old*, 2 vols. Berkeley: University of California Press.

Cortés, Hernán (1992) *Letters from Mexico*, ed. Anthony Pagden. New Haven, CT: Yale University Press.

Cro, Stelio (1994) 'Classical Antiquity, America and the Myth of the Noble Savage', in Haase and Meyer (1994), pp. 379–418.

Dickason, Olive Patricia (1988) 'Old World Law, New World Peoples, and Concepts of Sovereignty', in Palmer and Reinhartz (1988), pp. 52–78.

Doyle, Michael W. (1983) 'Kant, Liberal Legacies, and Foreign Affairs', *Philosophy and Public Affairs*, vol. 12, nos. 3 and 4, pp. 205–35, 323–53.

Echeverria, Durand (1956) *Mirage in the West. A History of the French Image of American Society to 1815*. Princeton, NJ: Princeton University Press.

Elliott, J. H. (1990) *Imperial Spain 1469–1716*. London: Penguin.

Englander, David, Diana Norman, Rosemary O'Day and W. R. Owens (eds) (1994) *Culture and Belief in Europe 1450–1600. An Anthology of Sources*. Oxford: Blackwell.

Erdheim, Mario (1982) 'Anthropologische Modelle des 16. Jahrhunderts. Über Las Casas, Oviedo und Sahagun', in Kohl (1982), pp. 57–67.

Ferguson, Adam (1995) *An Essay on the History of Civil Society*. Cambridge: Cambridge University Press.

Flint, Valerie I. J. (1992) *The Imaginative Landscape of Christopher Columbus*. Princeton, NJ: Princeton University Press.

Fukuyama, Francis (1989) 'The End of History?', *The National Interest*, Summer, pp. 3–18.

Geertz, Clifford (1993) *The Interpretation of Cultures*. London: Fontana Press.

Gilpin, Robert G. (1986) 'The Richness of the Tradition of Political Realism', in Keohane (1986), pp. 301–21.

Grisel, Etienne (1976) 'The Beginnings of International Law and the General Public Law Doctrine: Francisco de Vitoria's *De Indis Prior*', in Chiapelli (1976), pp. 305–25.

Grotius, Hugo (1925) *De Jure Belli Ac Pacis Libri Tres*. Oxford: Clarendon Press.

Grotius, Hugo (1950) *Vom Recht des Krieges und des Friedens*. Tübingen: Mohr.

Haase, Wolfgang and Reinhold Meyer (eds) (1994) *The Classical Tradition and the Americas*, vol. 1: *European Images of the Americas and the Classical Tradition*. Berlin and New York: Walter de Gruyter.

Hanke, Lewis (1964) *The First Social Experiments in America. A Study in the Development of Spanish Indian Policy in the Sixteenth Century*. Gloucester, MA: Peter Smith.

Hanke, Lewis (1974) *All Mankind is One. A Study of the Disputation Between Bartolomé de Las Casas and Juan Ginés de Sepúlveda in 1550 on the Intellectual and Religious Capacity of the American Indians*. DeKalb: Northern Illinois University Press.

Havens, George R. (1965) *The Age of Ideas. From Reaction to Revolution in Eighteenth-Century France*. New York: Free Press.

Hobbes, Thomas (1997) *Leviathan*. Cambridge: Cambridge University Press.

Hoffman, Stanley (1981) *Duties Beyond Borders. On the Limits and Possibilities of Ethical International Politics*. Syracuse, NY: Syracuse University Press.

Huntington, Samuel P. (1993) 'The Clash of Civilizations?', in *Foreign Affairs*, vol. 72, no. 3, pp. 22–49.

Iacono, Alfonso M. (1994) 'The American Indians and the Ancients of Europe: the Idea of Comparison and the Construction of Historical Time in the 18th Century', in Haase and Meyer (1994), pp. 658–81.

Jaenen, Cornelius J. (1988) 'Characteristics of French-Amerindian Contact in New France', in Palmer and Reinhartz (1988), pp. 79–101.

Kant, Immanuel (1993) *Schriften zur Anthropologie, Geschichtsphilosophie, Politik und Pädagogik I*. Frankfurt am Main: Suhrkamp.

Kant, Immanuel (1995) *Schriften zur Anthropologie, Geschichtsphilosophie, Politik und Pädagogik II*. Frankfurt am Main: Suhrkamp.

Kant, Immanuel (1996) *Political Writings*. Cambridge: Cambridge University Press.

Kautsky, Karl and Paul Lafargue (1968) *Vorläufer des neueren Sozialismus*, vol. 3. Hannover: Dietz.

Keohane, Robert O. (ed.) (1986) *Neorealism and its Critics*. New York: Columbia University Press.

Knutsen, Torbjørn L. (1992) *A History of International Relations Theory*. Manchester: Manchester University Press.

Kohl, Karl-Heinz (ed.) (1982) *Mythen der Neuen Welt. Zur Entdeckungsgeschichte Lateinamerikas*. Berlin: Frölich & Kaufmann.

Lafiteau, Joseph François (1977) *Customs of the American Indians Compared with the Customs of Primitive Times*, eds William N. Fenton and Elizabeth Moore, 2 vols. Toronto: Champlain Society.

Lange, Thomas (1982) 'Soutanenkaserne oder heiliges Experiment? Die Jesuitenreduktionen in Paraguay im europäischen Urteil', in Kohl (1982), pp. 210–23.

Las Casas, Bartolomé de (1971a) *History of the Indies*. New York: Harper & Row.

Las Casas, Barolomé de (1971b) *A Selection of His Writings*. ed. George Sanderlin. New York: Alfred A. Knopf.

Leed, Eric (1995) *Shores of Discovery. How Expeditionaries have Constructed the World*. New York: Basic Books.

Lestringant, Frank (1994) 'The Euhemerist Tradition and the European Perception and Description of the American Indians', in Haase and Meyer (1994), pp. 173–88.

Lewis, Gwynne (1993) *The French Revolution. Rethinking the Debate*. London: Routledge.

Locke, John (1994) *Two Treatises of Government*. Cambridge: Cambridge University Press.

Lyons, Oren and John Mohawk (eds) (1992) *Exiled in the Land of the Free. Democracy, Indian Nation, and the U.S. Constitution*. Santa Fe, NM: Clear Light Publishers.

McFarlane, Anthony (1994) *The British in the Americas 1480–1815*. London: Longman.

Mason, Peter (1990) *Deconstructing America – Representation of the Other*. London, New York: Routledge.

Mason Peter (1994) 'Classical Ethnography and Its Influence on the European Perception of the Peoples of the New World', in Haase and Meyer (1994), pp. 135–72.

Meek, Ronald L. (1976) *Social Science and the Ignoble Savage*. Cambridge: Cambridge University Press.

Moebus, Joachim (1982) 'Über die Bestimmung des Wilden und die Entwicklung des Verwertungsstandpunkts bei Kolumbus', in Kohl (1982), pp. 49–56.

Montaigne, Michel Eyquem de (1990) *The Essays*. Chicago: Encyclopaedia Britannica.

Montesquieu, Baron de (1949) *The Spirit of the Laws*. New York: Hafner Press.

More, Thomas (1993) *Utopia*. Cambridge: Cambridge University Press.

Morgenthau, Hans J. (1993) *Politics Among Nations. The Struggle for Power and Peace*, revised Kenneth W. Thompson. New York: McGraw-Hill.

Ninkovich, Frank (1990) 'Culture in US Foreign Policy', in Jongsuk Chay (ed.) *Culture and International Relations*. New York: Praeger.

Otruba, Gustav (1962) *Der Jesuitenstaat in Paraguay. Idee und Wirklichkeit*. Vienna.

Oviedo, G. F. de (1959) *Natural History of the West Indies*, ed. S. A. Stroudemire. Chapel Hill: University of North Carolina Studies.

Pagden, Anthony (1982) *The Fall of Natural Man. The American Indian and the Origins of Comparative Ethnology*. Cambridge: Cambridge University Press.

Pagden, Anthony (1990) *Spanish Imperialism and the Political Imagination. Studies in European and Spanish-American Social and Political Theory 1513–1830*. New Haven, CT, and London: Yale University Press.

Pagden, Anthony (1993) *European Encounters with the New World*. New Haven, CT, and London: Yale University Press.

Pagden, Anthony (1995) *Lords of All the World. Ideologies of Empire in Spain, Britain and France c.1500–c.1800*. New Haven, CT: Yale University Press.

Paine, Thomas (1995) *Rights of Man, Common Sense, and Other Political Writings*. Oxford: Oxford University Press.

Palmer, Stanley H. and Dennis Reinhartz (eds) (1988) *Essays on the History of North American Discovery and Exploration*. Arlington TX: Texas A+M University Press.

Parry, John H. (1976) 'A Secular Sense of Responsibility', in Chiapelli (1976), pp. 287–304.

Parry, John H. (1981) *The Age of Reconnaissance. Discovery, Exploration and Settlement 1450–1650*. Berkeley: University of California Press.

Parry, John H. (1990) *The Spanish Seaborne Empire*. Berkeley: University of California Press.

Pufendorf, Samuel von (1927) *De Officio Hominis et Civis Juxta Legem Naturalem Libri Duo*. New York: Oxford University Press.

Quinn, David B. (1988) 'Colonies in the Beginning: Examples from North America', in Palmer and Reinhartz (1988), pp. 10–34.

Raynal, Abbé (1969) *Philosophical and Political History of the Settlements and Trade of the Europeans in the East and West Indies*. New York: Negro University Press.

Rousseau, Jean-Jacques (1993) *The Social Contract and Discourses*. London: J. M. Dent.

Sahagun, Bernardino de (1978) *The War of Conquest: How it was Waged Here in Mexico: The Aztec's Own Story*. Salt Lake City: University of Utah Press.

Sánchez, Jean-Pierre (1994) 'Myths and Legends in the Old World and European Expansionism on the American Continent', in Haase and Meyer (1994), pp. 189–240.

Scammell, G. V. (1992) *The First Imperial Age. European Overseas Expansion c.1400–1715*. London: Routledge.

Scharlau, Birgit (1982) 'Beschreiben und Beherrschen. Die Informationspolitik der spanischen Krone im 15. und 16. Jahrhundert', in Kohl (1982), pp. 92–100.

Sepúlveda, Juan Ginés de (1994) 'On the Indians', in Englander et al. (1994), pp. 321–3.

Sheehan, Bernard W. (1980) *Savagism and Civility. Indians and Englishmen in Colonial Virginia*. Cambridge: Cambridge University Press.

Slavin, Arthur J. (1976) 'The American Principle from More to Locke', in Chiapelli (1976), pp. 139–64.

Smith, Adam (1989) *An Inquiry Into the Nature and Causes of the Wealth of Nations*. Chicago: Encyclopaedia Britannica.

Spicer, Edward H. (1992) *Cycles of Conquest. The Impact of Spain, Mexico, and the United States on the Indians of the Southwest, 1533–1960*. Tucson: University of Arizona Press.

Stanlis, Peter J. (1990) 'Edmund Burke, Jean-Jacques Rousseau, and the French Revolution', in Tonsor (ed.) (1990), pp. 41–70.

Stannard, David E. (1992) *American Holocaust. The Conquest of the New World*. New York: Oxford University Press.

Talmon, J. L. (1952) The Origins of Totalitarian Democracy. London: Heinemann.

Thomasius, Christian (1950) 'Vorrede von der Historie des Rechts der Natur bis auf Grotium', in Grotius (1950), pp. 1–28.

Tocqueville, Alexis de (1994) *Democracy in America*, 2 vols. London: David Campbell Publishers.

Todorov, Tzvetan (1999) *The Conquest of America. The Question of the Other*. Norman: University of Oklahoma Press.

Tonsor, Stephen J. (1990) 'Equality as a Factor in the American and French Revolutions', in Tonsor (ed.) (1990), pp. 114–37.

Tonsor, Stephen J. ed. (1990) *Reflections on the French Revolution*, Washington: Regnery Gateway.

Vattel, Emmerich de (1863) *The Law of Nations or Principles of the Law of Nature Applied to the Conduct and Affairs of Nations and Sovereigns.* Philadelphia: Johnson.

Venables, Robert W. (1992) 'American Indian Influences on the America of the Founding Fathers', in Lyons and Mohawk (1992), pp. 73–124.

Vitoria, Francisco de (1991) *Political Writings*, eds Anthony Pagden and Jeremy Lawrence. Cambridge: Cambridge University Press.

Waltz, Kenneth (1959) *Man, the State and War. A Theoretical Analysis.* New York: Columbia University Press.

Waltz, Kenneth (1979) *Theory of International Politics.* New York: McGraw-Hill.

Williams, Howard (1996) *International Relations and the Limits of Political Theory.* London: Macmillan.

Williams, Robert A. Jr (1992) *The American Indian in Western Legal Thought. The Discourses of Conquest.* New York: Oxford University Press.

Willson, John (1990) 'The Gods of Revolution', in Tonsor (ed.) (1990), pp. 20–40.

Wolff, Larry (1994) *Inventing Eastern Europe. The Map of Civilization on the Mind of the Enlightenment.* Stanford, CA: Stanford University Press.

Index